Questions to Ask Your Mormon Friend

Questions to Ask Your Mormon Friend

Challenging the Claims of Latter-day Saints in a Constructive Manner

BILL McKEEVER

ERIC JOHNSON

BETHANY HOUSE PUBLISHERS
MINNEAPOLIS, MINNESOTA 55438

Published by Bethany House Publishers
A Ministry of Bethany Fellowship, Inc.
11300 Hampshire Avenue South
Minneapolis, Minnesota 55438

Printed in the United States of America

Library of Congress Cataloging-in-Publication Data

McKeever, Bill.
    Questions to ask your Mormon friend / Bill McKeever & Eric
Johnson.
        p.   cm.

    1. Mormon Church—Controversial literature.   I. Johnson, Eric,
1962–   .   II. Title.
BX8645.M34   1994
289.3—dc20   94–16696
ISBN 1–55661–455–1   CIP

THANKS

Our utmost appreciation and affection to Tamar and Terri, two women who patiently survived their temporary position as "computer widows" while this book was being prepared. Thanks also to our good friends Dick Baer of Ex-Mormons and Christian Alliance, Marian Bodine at the Christian Research Institute, and Eric's 1993-94 Honors English-10 class at Christian High for their comments and input.

Mormonism Research Ministry is a Christian organization dedicated to informing the Body of Christ about the differences between Mormonism and biblical Christianity. Since 1979 MRM has been challenging the claims of Mormonism through its newsletter, tracts, books, tapes, and church presentations.

If you would like a free subscription to the quarterly publication *Mormonism Researched*, write:

> Mormonism Research Ministry
> Dept. Q
> P.O. Box 20705
> El Cajon, CA 92021

BILL McKEEVER is the author of *Answering Mormons' Questions* and director of Mormonism Research Ministry, a Christian apologetics organization based in southern California. His study of Mormon doctrine and history goes back to 1973.

ERIC JOHNSON received his M.Div. from Bethel Seminary West and has studied Mormonism since 1987. As an associate with Mormonism Research Ministry he has written a number of articles comparing Mormonism with biblical Christianity including the booklet *Quetzalcoatl—Jesus in the Americas?*

CONTENTS

INTRODUCTION

Mormon Apostle Orson Pratt made the following challenge in 1853 to those who were not persuaded that the Church of Jesus Christ of Latter-day Saints (referred to as the "LDS Church" or "Mormon Church" throughout this book) was the true church. He wrote:

> If we cannot convince you by reason nor by the word of God, that your religion is wrong, we will not persecute you, but will sustain you in the privileges, guaranteed in the great Charter of American Liberty: we ask from you the same generosity—protect us in the exercise of our religious rights—convince us of our errors of doctrine, if we have any, by reason, by logical arguments, or by the word of God, and we will be ever grateful for the information, and you will ever have the pleasing reflection that you have been instruments in the hands of God of redeeming your fellow beings from the darkness which you may see enveloping their minds.[1]

Many Christians have told us that, if they only knew what to say, they would be more than willing to talk with their Mormon acquaintances about their beliefs. Is there, they ask, some "magic question"

---

[1]Orson Pratt, *The Seer*, pp. 15–16.

that would supernaturally open up the spiritual eyes of sincere Mormons? We are sad to report that we do not know of any question that would fit that description.

However, there are a number of questions that a Christian can ask the Mormon who is a serious seeker after truth; these questions are intended to help the Latter-day Saint perceive the inconsistency of Mormonism. Unlike most books on the subject of Mormonism, the following chapters do not specifically function as a mere exposé or as a defense against Mormon accusations. Instead, our goal is to give you, the reader, information that can be used in a manner of offense and hopefully challenge the Latter-day Saints to seriously reexamine the doctrine that they have been led to believe is truth.

Before beginning this book, a word of caution is necessary. Extreme care is mandatory whenever taking the offensive position. While it is important to raise questions as Paul did on Mars Hill in Athens (see Acts 17), we do not need to offend the hearer. As with all witnessing opportunities, a Christ-like spirit must be exhibited. We must emulate the patience and compassion of our Lord Jesus Christ as well as His boldness.

As Christians, we cannot force anyone, including Mormons, to agree with our position. Our authority in Christ allows us to present the message; however, it is the place of the Holy Spirit to convict hearts and bring souls unto Christ. We need to be gracious. This may mean on some occasions to "agree to disagree" on a subject in order to keep communication lines and the relationship open. The Christian's role is to plant seeds and, if the opportunity arises, to reap a ready crop.

Avoid telling Mormons what they believe. Instead, ask them what their position is on a certain issue. Many Mormons who have converted from other churches joined the LDS Church with the misunderstanding that it was just another Christian denomination. If you are able to show them that their personal beliefs conflict with those of the LDS Church, they may be willing to take a closer inspection of their faith.

You will find that it is not at all uncommon to come across a Latter-day Saint who seems to have an answer for everything. However, it must be established whether or not the answer is: (1) biblical, (2) logical, or (3) in harmony with Mormon history and teachings. More often than not, the answer will fail in either one or more of these categories.

Make sure to define your terms. Many Bible-believing Christians have walked away from a conversation with a Mormon thinking that there was no difference between Mormonism and biblical Christianity. This is a common occurrence because Mormonism has adopted Christian terminology while substituting its private definitions. To help avoid this potential difficulty, a dictionary of the Mormon language has been provided at the end of this book. It is here that you will find terms used by both the Latter-day Saint and the Bible-believing Christian. Also included are LDS "buzz words," which are unique to Mormonism and may come up in a conversation.

Above all, it is important to be patient. It is easy to become frustrated. Remember, Mormonism is not an intellectual problem but rather a spiritual one. Because we are not wrestling with flesh and blood, it is important to realize that the Mormon is not the enemy. Bear in mind that "Mormonism" is more than just a set of doctrines. It is an entire social structure. To leave the LDS community can, for many Mormons, involve losing jobs, friends, and, at times, even families.

We would like to invite those readers who may be LDS to honestly evaluate the questions offered herein. We do not write as those who harbor hatred or animosity. Nor can our reasons be construed as "persecution." Rather, we hope you would agree that

> If a faith will not bear to be investigated; if its preachers and professors are afraid to have it examined, their foundation must be very weak.[2]

Using the formula of "reason, logical arguments, and the word of God," we take up the challenge of Orson Pratt.

---

[2]George A. Smith, first Counselor to Brigham Young, *Journal of Discourses* 14:216.

ONE

If I Accept You as a Christian, Will You Accept Me as a Mormon?

A sensitive topic to Mormons is whether or not Mormonism is a Christian religion. The Mormon's response may be like that of twelfth Mormon President Spencer W. Kimball when he said:

> Latter-day Saints are true Christians. We cannot understand how anyone could question our being Christians. It would certainly be a reflection upon anyone who would say such a thing, because if they attended even one session of any meeting of this church, they would come to realize that every prayer and every song and every sermon is centered in the Lord Jesus Christ. We are the true followers of Jesus Christ; and we hope the world will finally come to the conclusion that we are Christians, if there are any in the world.[1]

Mormon Apostle Bruce McConkie stated:

> Mormonism is Christianity; Christianity is Mormonism; they are one and the same, and they are not to be distinguished from each other in the minutest detail. . . . Mormons are true Chris-

---

[1]Edward L. Kimball, ed., *The Teachings of Spencer W. Kimball*, p. 434.

13

tians; their worship is the pure, unadulterated Christianity authored by Christ and accepted by Peter, James, and John and all the ancient saints.[2]

Rex Lee, the president of LDS-owned Brigham Young University, felt that it was "ridiculous" to not consider Mormons as Christians. He added:

> I assume that qualification as a Christian turns mainly on a belief in Christ. Mormons not only qualify as Christians under that definition, but they have also given broader meaning to the definition itself.[3]

The LDS Church has been striving in recent years to gain acceptance as a Christian religion. Although the LDS Church has been very successful at polishing its image, it has never backed off from its many heretical doctrines, which distinguish it from biblical Christianity. While many Mormons claim that they should also be entitled to the name of "Christian," many of these same Mormons would be equally offended if Bible-believing Christians insisted on being called "Mormons."

Imagine the Mormons' reaction to the following statement:

I'm a Mormon but I don't believe Joseph Smith was a true prophet of God. I'm a Mormon but I don't believe that God was once a man or that men can become gods. I'm a Mormon but I don't believe the Mormon Church is the only true church or that we need human prophets to guide the church. I'm a Mormon but I don't believe the *Book of Mormon* is the Word of God. I'm a Mormon but I don't believe temples are necessary or that couples can be married for eternity.

A knowledgeable Latter-day Saint would defy that such a person was, in fact, a true Mormon. Why? Because this person who claims to be Mormon denies the very doctrines that make Mormons what they are. At the same time, however, a Mormon who claims to be Christian denies the very doctrines that make Christians what they are.

Indeed, Mormonism denies or distorts the basic tenets of biblical Christianity. The two religions are incompatible. The areas of differ-

[2]Bruce R. McConkie, *Mormon Doctrine*, p. 513.
[3]Rex Lee, *What Do Mormons Believe?* p. 19.

ence include the doctrine of God, the basis for authority, and the idea of salvation for mankind.

Brigham Young University professors Daniel C. Peterson and Stephen D. Ricks ask "anti-Mormons" to refrain from calling Mormonism a cult. They ask that "more neutral terminology [be used], such as 'religious movement,' 'religious group,' or 'church.' "[4] We would be most willing to do this (as we have throughout this book), but in return we would ask the Mormon Church to quit attempting to use the name "Christian" to describe its "religious movement."

Unlike many contemporary Mormons who desire to have equal status within Christianity, many LDS leaders have gone out of their way to deride these same Christian churches. Throughout the history of the LDS Church, its leaders have continually taught that Mormonism is far superior to the Christian denominations.

Joseph Smith, Jr., the founder of Mormonism, made the first attack on Christianity when he claimed to have asked God, in 1820, which of all the churches was correct. He was answered that "I must join none of them, for they were all wrong; and the Personage who addressed me said that all their creeds were an abomination in His sight; that those professors were all corrupt. . . ."[5]

According to Smith, Christianity was not in need of a *reformation*. Rather, its corruption was so severe that a complete *restoration* was necessary. Drs. Peterson and Ricks attempted to downplay the severity of Christianity's depravity by claiming that Smith merely referred to the local churches at the time of his youth. They write:

> What the Lord told Joseph Smith in the grove was that the churches and creeds of 1820 were defective and distorted by error. He did not say that they were entirely and utterly wrong (since they preserved much truth), nor did he say that each and every Christian church would always be wrong. . . . He did not say that Christianity, as such, is false. There is nothing logically wrong with saying that the churches of 1820 were incorrect on many important issues ("corrupt"), and then saying that The Church of Jesus Christ of Latter-day Saints (organized in 1830) is true.[6]

---

[4]Dr. Daniel C. Peterson and Dr. Stephen D. Ricks, *Offenders for a Word: How Anti-Mormons Play Word Games to Attack the Latter-day Saints*, p. 211.
[5]*Joseph Smith's Testimony* 1:19.
[6]Peterson and Ricks, *Offenders for a Word*, pp. 170–171.

Was Smith really referring only to the churches of 1820? To draw such a conclusion undermines the very existence of the LDS Church as well as goes against the pronounced statements of many Mormon leaders. Contrary to what these professors claim, Bruce McConkie seems to be more consistent with Mormonism's overall attack on Christianity. Following a quotation of the Athanasian Creed, he concluded:

> Is it any wonder that the Lord of heaven, as He stood by His Father's side on that glorious day in 1820, speaking of *all* the churches in *all* Christendom, told young Joseph "that *all* their creeds were an abomination in his sight"?[7]

What Smith supposedly was told by God—that there could only be one true church upon the earth—is supported by the *Book of Mormon* itself. It reads:

> And he said unto me: Behold there are save two churches only; the one is the church of the Lamb of God, and the other is the church of the devil; wherefore, whoso belongeth not to the church of the Lamb of God belongeth to that great church, which is the mother of abominations; and she is the whore of all the earth.[8]

McConkie described the "church of the devil" when he wrote:

> What is the church of the devil in our day, and where is the seat of her power?. . . . It is all of the systems, both *Christian* and non-Christian, that perverted the pure and perfect gospel. . . . It is communism; it is Islam; it is Buddhism; *it is modern Christianity in all its parts.* It is Germany under Hitler, Russia under Stalin, and Italy under Mussolini.[9]

Doctrine and Covenants 1:30 confirms this idea of exclusivity when it says that Smith's restored church is "the only true and living church upon the face of the whole earth, with which I, the Lord, am well pleased. . . ." Expounding on the idea that only two churches exist—the Church of the Lamb and the Church of Babylon—George Q. Cannon, a former member of the LDS First Presidency, said:

---

[7]McConkie, *The Promised Messiah*, p. 117, (emphasis ours).
[8]1 Nephi 14:10.
[9]McConkie, *The Millennial Messiah*, pp. 54–55, (emphasis ours).

The various organizations which *are* called churches through-out Christendom, though differing in their creeds and organiza-tions, have one common origin. They all belong to Babylon. God is not the founder of them, yet there are many sincere people who belong to them. These the Elders of the Church are commanded to warn, and they are commanded to gather out. The Spirit of the Lord moves upon the people who will listen to His servants to leave Babylon and join the Church of the Lamb.[10]

Cannon also wrote:

"Mormonism". . . is either true or false; if true, it is every man's duty to obey it; if false, it is every man's prerogative to know its falsity. We say it is true. . . . We say it will have to be believed and obeyed by all men, or they will be condemned.[11]

As indicated by the present tense of his statement, Cannon be-lieved any non-LDS church is part of Babylon or, as the *Book of Mormon* puts it, "the church of the devil."

Further evidence for the low opinion of Christianity held by these leaders comes from the *Journal of Discourses* including:

- Second LDS President Brigham Young who said Christians "are groveling in darkness."[12] He believed the "professing Christian world [is] like a ship upon a boisterous ocean without rudder, compass, or pilot . . . tossed hither and thither by every wind of doctrine."[13] All but Mormons will be damned.[14] Young explained the reason why Christianity differs from Mormonism when he said, "It is simply because they are not Christians as the New Testament defines Christianity."[15]

- Apostle Heber C. Kimball who stated, "Christians—those poor, mis-erable priests Brother Brigham was speaking about—some of them are the biggest whoremasters there are on the earth. . . ."[16] He also felt that "the curse of God shall be upon" anyone who rejected the Mormon God or his cause.[17]

---

[10]George Q. Cannon, *Gospel Truth*, p. 324, (emphasis ours).
[11]Ibid., p. 297.
[12]*Journal of Discourses* 5:73.
[13]*Journal of Discourses* 10:265.
[14]*Journal of Discourses* 11:271.
[15]*Journal of Discourses* 10:230.
[16]*Journal of Discourses* 5:89.
[17]*Journal of Discourses* 6:38.

- Apostle Orson Pratt who claimed that: "Both Catholics and Protestants are nothing less than the '*whore of Babylon*' whom the Lord denounces. . . . And any person who shall be so wicked as to receive a holy ordinance of the gospel from the ministers of any of these apostate churches will be sent down to hell with them, unless they repent of the unholy and impious act."[18]

These are several early leaders who did not accept Christianity as being complete and therefore not having the same authority as Mormonism. In response to whether or not the LDS Church had "a monopoly on truth," Mormon Apostle John A. Widtsoe replied:

> Only the Church possessing this authority is the complete Church of Christ, and there can be but one. All others lack the necessary authority and are therefore incomplete. The Church of Jesus Christ of Latter-day Saints posesses (sic) the full truth relative to the gospel of the Lord Jesus Christ, the one divine plan of salvation, and also the authority to officiate in God's name in the upbuilding of the Church of Christ. There is but one gospel; there can be but one Priesthood; there is but one Church which encompasses the whole truth of the gospel, and into which all truth may find its place. In that sense the Church claims to possess the full fundamental truth, call it monopoly if you choose, necessary for full salvation in the celestial kingdom of God. This the Church does humbly and gratefully, keenly sensible of its high commission and vast responsibility, to lead all mankind into a fulness of the knowledge leading to eternal progression in the presence of the Lord.[19]

Tenth Mormon President Joseph Fielding Smith adamantly agreed with Widtsoe's assessment, adding:

> A man cannot receive the fulness of truth except in the kingdom of God, in other words, if you please, the Church of Jesus Christ of Latter-day Saints. *No man*—no matter how great his education, no matter how much he studies in the things of the world, no matter what he does in the eternities to come—*will ever reach the goal of perfection in truth or the fulness of light and understanding outside of the kingdom of God.*[20]

---

[18]Pratt, *The Seer*, p. 255, (emphasis his).
[19]John A. Widtsoe, *Evidences and Reconciliations*, p. 24.
[20]Joseph Fielding Smith, *Doctrines of Salvation* 1:299, (emphasis his).

He taught that the celestial kingdom is for those who "abide in the fulness of the gospel of Jesus Christ," meaning it is reserved for the Mormons.[21]

Bruce McConkie, Smith's son-in-law, emphasized that full truth could not be found in "the unorganized spiritual vagary termed the Christian Church by sectarianism." He wrote:

> Christianity is the religion of the Christians. Hence, true and acceptable Christianity is found among the saints who have the fulness of the gospel, and a perverted Christianity holds sway among the so-called Christians of apostate Christendom.[22]

To be sure he was not misunderstood, McConkie also said:

> And virtually all the millions of apostate Christendom have abased themselves before the mythical throne of a mythical Christ. . . . In large part the worship of apostate Christendom is performed in ignorance, as much so as was the worship of the Athenians who bowed before the Unknown God. . . .[23]

Claiming that "there is no salvation outside this one true Church," McConkie added:

> To his earthly kingdom in the dispensation of the fulness of times the Lord has given the formal name, The Church of Jesus Christ of Latter-day Saints. (D & C 115:3–4.) This Church is "the only true and living church upon the face of the whole earth" (D & C 1:30), the only organization authorized by the Almighty to preach his gospel and administer the ordinances of salvation, the only Church which has power to save and exalt men in the hereafter. Membership in this divine institution is a pearl of great price.[24]

Mormon Apostle Boyd K. Packer agreed with these past leaders and made it clear that if the Christian faith is to be united, it must be under the banner of Mormonism. He wrote:

> In obedience we remain independent. While we cooperate with others to reach mutual objectives, we do it in our own way. We do

---

[21]Ibid., 2:25.
[22]McConkie, *Mormon Doctrine*, p. 132.
[23]Ibid., pp. 269, 374.
[24]Ibid., pp. 136, 138.

not recognize the ordinances performed in other churches. We will not exchange baptisms. . . . We do not join associations of clergy or councils of churches. We keep our distance from the ecumenical movements. The restored gospel is the means by which Christians must ultimately be united.[25]

Rex Lee added:

Complete ecumenism would require either that The Church of Jesus Christ of Latter-day Saints deny its divine authority or that others in the ecumenical movement accept it, neither of which is possible.[26]

Although Packer said that the LDS Church officially stays away from the "ecumenical movements," unofficially many Mormons are befriending Christians in an attempt to convert them to Mormonism. For instance, Mormon author Darl Andersen developed a seminar for Mormons entitled "Win a Minister and Influence a Thousand." While Andersen's intent to "friendship" may appear to be a gesture of good-will, he admitted to having underlying motives:

Some LDS question the integrity of making friends with ministers while "out after their sheep". . . . Only those who do not comprehend this fact should question the integrity involved. . . .[27]

Andersen gave possible strategies such as visiting Christian ministers at their churches, inviting them to lunch, and having joint Thanksgiving services.

Meanwhile, Peterson and Ricks claim "conservative Protestants" are practically the only Christians who would not allow Mormons into their ecumenical fellowships. They wrote:

Indeed, perhaps the greatest irony of the current campaign against Mormonism is that it is almost entirely the work of conservative Protestant Christians. Latter-day Saints have long tended to feel at home with evangelical Bible commentaries, when they use such scholarly tools at all, because of the belief that we share with them in Christ's literal resurrection, in the historicity of his mir-

---

[25]*The Ensign*, November 1985, p. 82.
[26]Lee, *What Do Mormons Believe?* p. 83.
[27]From seminar notes.

acles, in the birth narratives, and in the Savior's divinity.[28]

It is true that some churches—such as liberal denominations and other groups which place ecumenicism above doctrinal purity—allow the LDS Church to gain credibility by accepting it as a sister organization. Any agreement with LDS doctrine would tend to be in a generic sense. While Christians and Mormons may believe in Christ's literal resurrection, Christians do not believe that Jesus went to the Americas after His resurrection, nor that His resurrection merely paves the way for men to be resurrected; they do not hold that Christ's birth was a result of God the Father having sexual relations with Mary;[29] nor do Christians believe that Jesus is a created being who was the spirit-brother of Lucifer.[30]

Christians have never worshiped a God who, as the offspring of another God, became a mortal man and eventually attained godhood.[31] They have also never worshiped a being who resides near a planet called Kolob.[32]

Peterson and Ricks also wrote:

> At least until recently, Mormons have thought of conservative Christians as, in many ways, their allies. . . . Most Latter-day Saints can only shake their heads, therefore, at the claim that Mormonism is not Christian.[33]

Despite the arguments made by these writers, Gordon B. Hinckley, first counselor to LDS President Ezra Taft Benson, disagreed that the differences are minor. Speaking of the uniqueness of his church while classifying it as Christian, he wrote the following in an LDS Church tract:

> They [Mormons] are generally classed as Protestants, since they

---

[28]Peterson and Ricks, *Offenders for a Word*, p. 57.
[29]*Gospel Principles*, p. 57; McConkie, *Mormon Doctrine*, pp. 547, 742; Benson, *The Teachings of Ezra Taft Benson*, p. 7; *Journal of Discourses* 8:115; Pratt, *The Seer*, p. 158; *Family Home Evening Manual*, 1972, pp. 125–126; J. F. Smith, *Doctrines of Salvation* 1:18.
[30]*Gospel Principles*, p. 15; Kimball, editor, *The Teachings of Spencer W. Kimball*, pp. 33–34; Milton R. Hunter, *The Gospel Through the Ages*, p. 15.
[31]Joseph Fielding Smith, editor, *Teachings of the Prophet Joseph Smith*, pp. 345–346.
[32]Book of Abraham 3:3–18.
[33]Peterson and Ricks, *Offenders for a Word*, p. 57.

are not Catholics. Actually they are no closer to Protestantism than they are to Catholicism. Neither historically nor on the basis of modern association, theology, or practice, can they be grouped with either. . . . Suffice it to say that its theology, its organization, and its practices are in many respects entirely unique among today's Christian denominations.[34]

Mormon leaders since Joseph Smith's day have continually emphasized the differences, not the similarities, between Mormonism and Christianity. A Christian who is approached by a Mormon who says Mormonism is "just the same" as biblical Christianity needs to realize that this Mormon either does not know Mormonism or does not know the tenets of the Christian faith.

---

[34]From the LDS pamphlet *What of the Mormons?* p. 2.

T W O

Which First Vision Account Should We Believe?

Mormons are taught that, as a fourteen-year-old young man, Joseph Smith was visited by both God the Father and Jesus Christ during the spring of 1820. This visitation is known in Mormon circles as the "first vision."

According to the official LDS version, Smith was perplexed by the behavior of certain Christians in the area where he lived. He stated that, in 1820, there was a "religious excitement on the subject of religion," and that this revival ended with the various Christian denominations quarreling over where the converts would attend church.[1]

Because of the "confusion and strife among the different denominations,"[2] Smith wondered who was right and who was wrong. It was while reading James 1:5 that he decided to pray about the matter.[3] He proceeded to kneel down and pray among some nearby trees at a place that is known today as the Sacred Grove; it was here Smith claimed to have been visited by the two personages.

---

[1] *Joseph Smith History* 1:5.
[2] Ibid., 1:8.
[3] Ibid., 1:11.

23

When he asked the personages "which of all the sects was right," Smith said he was told that they were all wrong, that their creeds were an abomination in God's sight, and that all the professors of those creeds were corrupt.[4] There is little question that this statement was a direct assault on all of Christianity, not just the small congregations in the Palmyra area (New York) where Smith lived, which is what some Mormons have been led to believe.

The reason the aforementioned account has been referred to as the "official" version is because this is not the only description of the story. Thus, the question remains: If any of the accounts should be believed, which should it be?

To say the first vision story is just "another" event within the history of Mormonism is an understatement. McConkie wrote:

> This vision was the most important event that had taken place in all world history from the day of Christ's ministry to the glorious hour when it occurred.[5]

According to former LDS Apostle LeGrand Richards:

> On the morning of a beautiful spring day in 1820 there occurred one of the most important and momentous events in this world's history. God, the Eternal Father and His Son, Jesus Christ, appeared to Joseph Smith and gave instructions concerning the establishment of the kingdom of God upon the earth in these latter days.[6]

This vision is significant to a Mormon for a number of reasons, the two major ones being: Latter-day Saints have used this event to support the notion that God the Father and Jesus Christ, as two separate and distinct personages, are also two distinct and separate gods. And two, it gives the Mormon justification to believe Christianity had fallen into a complete apostasy and needed to be restored to earth.

Why are there so many different accounts of this story? Many early Mormon leaders gave conflicting versions of Smith's experience. For instance, Smith's successor, Brigham Young, said the young Smith was visited by an angel:

---

[4]Ibid., 1:18,19.
[5]McConkie, *Mormon Doctrine*, p. 285.
[6]LeGrand Richards, *A Marvelous Work and a Wonder*, p. 7.

The Lord did not come with the armies of heaven, in power and great glory, nor send His messengers panoplied with aught else than the truth of heaven, to communicate to the meek, the lowly, the youth of humble origin, the sincere enquirer after the knowledge of God. But He did send His angel to this same obscure person, Joseph Smith jun., who afterwards became a Prophet, Seer, and Revelator, and informed him that he should not join any of the religious sects of the day, for they were all wrong; that they were following the precepts of men instead of the Lord Jesus Christ.[7]

Some Mormons may assert that Young was referring to Smith's visitation by the angel Moroni in 1823; this is doubtful since Smith never asked Moroni which of the churches was right during this supposed visitation. In fact, there would have been no reason to have asked such a question since this was answered in the Sacred Grove three years earlier.

George A. Smith, first counselor to Brigham Young,[8] said Joseph Smith was not visited by either the Father and/or the Son or by an individual angel. Rather, Smith was visited by a multitude of angels:

Joseph Smith had attended these meetings, and when this result was reached he saw clearly that something was wrong . . . he went humbly before the Lord and inquired of Him, and the Lord answered his prayer, and revealed to Joseph, by the ministrations of angels, the true condition of the world. When the holy angel appeared, Joseph inquired which of all these denominations was right and which he should join, and was told they were all wrong, they had all gone astray. . . .[9]

Clouding the issue even further is the fact that both Apostles Orson Pratt and Orson Hyde claimed Smith was visited by two identical personages, neither of which is described as being God the Father or Jesus Christ. Mormon author Milton V. Backman stated that Pratt's account is the "first known publication of the First Vision."[10] Pratt said Smith "saw two glorious personages, who exactly resembled each other in their features or likeness." Hyde gives a similar account but

[7]*Journal of Discourses* 2:171.
[8]Smith should not be confused with George A. Smith, the eighth president of the LDS Church.
[9]*Journal of Discourses* 12:334.
[10]Backman, *Joseph Smith's First Vision*, p. 170.

adds that the personages told Smith that "the Lord had decided to grant him a special blessing."[11] The use of the third person shows it was not the Lord who showed up.

Joseph Smith's 1832 diary also conflicts with the official account found in modern editions of the *Pearl of Great Price*. Backman stated that this is the earliest known account of Smith's first vision.[12] In this narrative, Smith claims to have been sixteen years old instead of fifteen.[13] In his 1832 diary account, reprinted as closely to the original as possible, Smith wrote:

> . . . and while in the attitude of calling upon the Lord in the 16th year of my age a piller of ~~fire~~ light above the brightness of the sun at noon day come down from above and rested upon me and I was filld with the spirit of God, and the Lord opened the heavens upon me and I saw the Lord and he spake unto me saying Joseph my son Thy Sins are forgiven thee. go thy way walk in my statutes and keep my commandments . . . behold I am the Lord of glory I was crucifyed for the world. . . .[14]

It is interesting to note in this version how Smith never said that he was visited by God the Father. While he does mention that there were certain people who drew near to God with their lips while their hearts remained far from Him, he was not told that all the churches were wrong, that their creeds were an abomination, and that their professors were corrupt. Despite these inconsistencies, the LDS Church took it upon itself to promote an account that was written eighteen years after the fact.[15]

A close examination of the official account leaves a number of unanswered questions. For instance, in versions printed before 1981, Smith claimed that his brother Alvin "died November 19th, 1824, in the 27th year of his age."[16] However, Smith's personal account was modified more than a century after Joseph Smith died. Editions

---

[11]Ibid., pp. 172, 175.

[12]Ibid., p. 155.

[13]If the Palmyra revival actually took place in the spring of 1820, Smith would have been fourteen and a half years old. Oliver Cowdery states in the *Times and Seasons* 2:241 that Smith was seventeen at the time and that the date was 1823.

[14]*Joseph Smith's 1832 Account of His Early Life*, p. 7.

[15]*Joseph Smith History* 1:2.

[16]*Joseph Smith 2*, 1:4; 1977 edition.

printed after 1981 state that Alvin died "November 19th, *1823*, in the *26th* year of his age." Both accounts disagree with Alvin's headstone which is still located in a small graveyard in Palmyra. The headstone concurs with the post–1981 editions regarding the date of his death, but his gravemarker says he was twenty-five years old, not twenty-six.

Joseph Smith claimed the confusion that ended the 1820 revival caused him to wonder if all the parties involved were wrong; he claimed later that it never entered into his heart that all the sects were wrong.[17]

While Smith wrote that this "religious excitement" caused "great multitudes" to be added to the churches,[18] the statistics of that time do not support this claim. Research performed by the late Christian pastor/researcher Wesley Walters shows there was no revival at all in Palmyra, N.Y. in 1820. The Presbyterian church records give no indication of an 1820 revival while the Baptist church in Palmyra showed an increase of only six members. Walters stated that the Methodist Church, "though referring to the entire circuit," showed a net loss of six members in 1820.[19]

The official LDS account states that Smith was visited on September 23, 1823, by an angel named Moroni, yet in his 1832 diary he claims this event took place on September 22, 1822.

Even the name of the angel has gone through a revision. In the official account, Smith says it was an angel named Moroni who visited him, yet Smith changed the name of this angel as late as 1842. Both the *Times and Seasons* 3:753 and the first edition of the *Pearl of Great Price* quote Smith as saying the name of the angel was Nephi, not Moroni. It was this angel who supposedly appeared to Smith in 1823 and told him about the gold plates, which contained a record of the former inhabitants of the American continent. These were said to have been hidden in a hill not far from the Smith farm.[20]

Smith said the plates measured six inches wide, eight inches long, and that the volume was nearly six inches thick. Each plate was about as thick as common tin.[21] Few Mormons dispute Smith's claim that he dug the plates out of the earth and carried them to his home three

---

[17]*Joseph Smith History* 1:18.
[18]Ibid., 1:5.
[19]Wesley Walters, *New Light on Mormon Origins*, p. 12.
[20]*Joseph Smith History* 1:34.
[21]*Documentary History of the Church* 4:537.

miles away. Joseph Smith's mother, Lucy Mack Smith, describes the event as follows:

> Joseph, on coming to them [the plates], took them from their secret place, and, wrapping them in his linen frock, placed them under his arm and started for home. After proceeding a short distance, he thought it would be more safe to leave the road and go through the woods. Traveling some distance after he left the road, he came to a large windfall, and as he was jumping over a log, a man sprang up from behind it and gave him a heavy blow with a gun. Joseph turned around and knocked him down, then ran at the top of his speed. About half a mile farther he was attacked again in the same manner as before; he knocked this man down in like manner as the former and ran on again; and before he reached home he was assaulted the third time. In striking the last one, he dislocated his thumb, which, however, he did not notice until he came within sight of the house, when he threw himself down in the corner of the fence in order to recover his breath. As soon as he was able, he arose and came to the house. He was still altogether speechless from fright and the fatigue of running.[22]

This story also raises a number of questions. How could Joseph Smith carry such a heavy load of plates and be able to run, jump, and fight off attackers? If the plates were the size claimed by Smith, they would have weighed at least 100 pounds. Tucking such a heavy object under the arm of even the strongest of young men is hard to imagine. To do this while jumping over logs, fighting off attackers, and running at top speed is Herculean.

The Foundation for Ancient Research and Mormon Studies (F.A.R.M.S.) provides bulletin covers containing information on the *Book of Mormon* on the back page. One article suggests that the plates might not have been gold after all. It theorizes that the plates may have been composed of an alloy called tumbaga consisting of 8k gold and copper since "pure gold would be too soft to make useful plates."[23]

---

[22]*History of Joseph Smith by His Mother, Lucy Mack Smith*, p. 108.

[23]F.A.R.M.S. bulletin cover entitled, "Were the 'Golden' Plates Gold?" The argument that plates of pure gold would have been too soft questions the validity of Mosiah 8:9. This passage in the *Book of Mormon* tells of twenty-four Jaredite plates "which are filled with engravings, and they are of pure gold." The article describes tumbaga as being naturally red in color, which turns to a golden color when treated with a simple acid.

To support the tumbaga theory, the article quotes William Smith, Joseph Smith's brother, who said the plates were a mixture of gold and copper.[24] One can only imagine how William arrived at such a conclusion since there is no evidence to suggest that the plates were ever analyzed. Making William's statement even less credible is the fact that he admitted to having never seen the plates:

> I was permitted to lift them as they laid in a pillow-case; but not to see them, as it was contrary to the commands he had received. They weighed about sixty pounds according to the best of my judgement.[25]

If the plates were really made of tumbaga, why didn't the angel say, "There was a book deposited, written upon *copper* plates, giving an account of the former inhabitants of this continent?" Because 8k means the metal was only about 33% gold, it probably would have been more correct to say the plates were copper, since roughly 66% of the plates would be composed of that metal.

To support the idea of records being made on gold plates, many past editions of the *Book of Mormon* included a picture of a "gold tablet found in Persia in 1961, dating to the time of Darius II." In his book *An Approach to the Book of Mormon*, Dr. Hugh Nibley draws a parallel to "pure plates of gold" written by "Darius the Median."[26] If the plates deposited by Moroni were really an alloy composed mostly of copper, why did the Mormon Church and Dr. Nibley draw parallels with plates of gold?

It would seem that William Smith's testimony concerning the plates would be offset by that of David Whitmer, since Whitmer was one of the few people who was supposedly authorized to see the plates found by Smith. In 1878, the *Saints' Herald* published a letter which stated:

> Mr. Whitmer stated that he had often handled the identical golden plates that Mr. Smith received from the hand of the angel; he said it was of pure gold, part of the book was sealed up solid, the other part was open and it was this part which was translated,

---

[24]The article gives no reference for William's statement; however, this comment is found in the *Saints' Herald*, 31 (1884), p. 644.
[25]Francis W. Kirkham, *A New Witness for Christ in America*, Vol. 2, p. 417.
[26]Dr. Hugh Nibley, *An Approach to the Book of Mormon*, 1978 edition, p. 19.

and is termed today the Mormon Bible.[27]

The F.A.R.M.S. article states that tumbaga plates would have weighed only about 53 pounds. Still, this would be like casually carrying a small sack of redi-mix cement under one's arm. This is not a very simple task!

In his testimony, Joseph Smith states that he was called a money-digger because he helped a man by the name of Josiah Stoal dig for a silver mine.[28] The truth of the matter is that Smith's dubious distinction as a money-digger arose from his claim that he could find buried treasure using a magical peep-stone. This occupation would eventually land Smith in court. Former Mormon historian D. Michael Quinn stated:

> For many years Mormon writers denied that such a court case occurred despite contrary evidence. A newspaper article in 1831 claimed that about 1826 or 1827 a court tried Smith "as a disorderly person" because "he was about the country in the character of a glasslooker: pretending to discover lost goods, hidden treasures, mines of gold and silver, etc."[29]

To prove that Joseph Smith was a charlatan would certainly cast doubt on his character and position as a prophet of God. Mormon writer Francis Kirkham appears to have understood this when he wrote:

> If any evidence had been in existence that Joseph Smith had used a seer stone for fraud and deception, and especially had he made this confession in a court of law as early as 1826, or four years before the Book of Mormon was printed, and his confession was in a court record, it would have been impossible for him to have organized the restored Church.[30]

Again, thanks to Wesley Walters, the court records from 1826 have been discovered to show that Smith was arrested, tried, and convicted for using this stone in his scam operations.[31]

---

[27]Letter by I. C. Funn printed in the *Saints' Herald*, February 15, 1878, p. 57.
[28]*Joseph Smith History* 1:56.
[29]Michael D. Quinn, *Early Mormonism and the Magic World View*, p. 44.
[30]*A New Witness for Christ in America* 1:387.
[31]Wesley Walters, *Joseph Smith's Bainbridge, N.Y., Court Trials*.

Such conflicting testimony about the different accounts would not make a strong case in a court of law. This is one reason why the LDS Church would rather have prospective converts search for truth through subjective feelings rather than objective evidence.

THREE

How Do You Determine Doctrinal Truth?

The search for truth has been the object of mankind since the dawn of time. When the Lord Jesus stood before an angry crowd in Pilate's judgment hall, the Roman procurator asked Him, "What is truth?"[1] For centuries Christians have found truth in the person and words of Jesus Christ. The Lord made it very clear that He alone was the way, the truth, and the life, and that no person could know the Father except through Him.[2]

In His great intercessory prayer for His disciples, Jesus asked the Father to sanctify them through His truth because His words were truth.[3] God has revealed His Word in the Bible, the standard by which Christians determine right from wrong and truth from error.

Jesus also warned that a day would come when some impostors would claim to be Christs, or anointed ones, and deceive many people into believing that they alone had truth. They would purposely undermine the standard to determine truth and set forth new guidelines. This is exactly what Mormonism has done.

---

[1]John 18:38.
[2]John 14:6.
[3]John 17:17.

Throughout its history, Mormonism has given conflicting rules by which to judge truth. Like many Christians, Joseph Smith began his quest for truth by turning to the Bible (James 1:5). Sadly, however, he ignored the many other passages from the Bible which would have warned him that his visitation in the "sacred grove" was anything but a manifestation from God.

The Standard Works

Most Mormons are led to believe that doctrinal truth can only come from Mormonism's standard works: the Bible, the *Book of Mormon*, the *Doctrine and Covenants*, and the *Pearl of Great Price*. Proponents of this view feel that this excuses them from the many embarrassing comments brought about by past leaders, including Mormonism's founder Joseph Smith, second president Brigham Young, and others. Since many of these statements are found in writings outside the standard works, these particular Latter-day Saints feel such comments are not worth entertaining since they are not considered church doctrine.

Although it may appear on the surface that all Mormons would agree with each other when it comes to particular doctrines, anyone who has spent a substantial amount of time talking about theological issues with Mormons knows that this is not the case. Such experience will show that there is wide diversity among Latter-day Saints regarding what is and what is not "Mormon doctrine." If a Mormon carefully took inventory of the doctrines making up his/her faith, the person would probably discover that many of them cannot be supported by the standard works. For instance, consider the teaching of a heavenly mother. Where in the standard works is the teaching that there is a "mother in heaven" who is married to God? Mormon Apostle Bruce McConkie admits this is an "unspoken truth."[4] Instead of turning to the standard works, McConkie refers to outside sources.

If true doctrine must be found in the standard works, where are the specific instructions regarding the LDS temple endowment ceremony? This is probably one of the most important elements pertaining to a Mormon's progression to godhood, yet the temple endowment ceremony is not in the standard works.

---

[4]McConkie, *Mormon Doctrine*, p. 516.

Most people would be suspicious of any person who claimed that the sun was inhabited,[5] that gold and silver grow like wheat in the field,[6] and that Adam was God;[7] yet, second LDS President Brigham Young taught all these things as factual, and he is still considered by Latter-day Saints to be a true prophet.

Tenth LDS President Joseph Fielding Smith wrote:

> It makes no difference what is written or what anyone has said, if what has been said is in conflict with what the Lord has revealed, we can set it aside. My words, and the teachings of any other member of the Church, high or low, if they do not square with the revelations, we need not accept them. Let us have the matter clear. We have accepted the four standard works as the measuring yardsticks, or balances, by which we measure every man's doctrine.[8]

Smith makes it clear that true doctrine can only be found in the standard works. Anything that contradicts its contents must be classified as spurious. Mormonism's eleventh president Harold B. Lee concurred with his predecessor when he declared:

> If it is not in the standard works, we may well assume that it is speculation, man's own personal opinion; and if it contradicts what is in the scriptures, it is not true. This is the standard by which we measure all truth.[9]

Brigham Young University professor Stephen E. Robinson took a similar position:

> Of course it is true that many Latter-day Saints, from the Presidents of the Church and members of the Quorum of the Twelve down to individual members who may write books or articles, have expressed their own opinions on doctrinal matters. Nevertheless, until such opinions are presented to the Church in general conference and sustained by vote of the conference, they are neither binding nor the official doctrine of the Church.[10]

Amazingly, Dr. Robinson defends the many blunders of past LDS

---

[5]*Journal of Discourses* 13:271.
[6]Ibid., 1:219.
[7]Ibid., 1:50.
[8]Joseph Fielding Smith, *Doctrines of Salvation* 3:203.
[9]*Improvement Era*, January 1969, p. 13.
[10]Stephen E. Robinson, *Are Mormons Christian?* p. 15.

leaders by quoting Joseph Smith who said:

> I told them that a prophet was a prophet only when he was
> acting as such.[11]

For Robinson to quote Smith from a book which is not considered
to be part of the standard works is an example of circular reasoning.
It is inconsistent because the quote used by Robinson is not found in
the standard works and was not given in a conference speech. Even
if Smith did say this at a conference, it was not voted upon. In fact,
the idea that "a prophet is a prophet only when he [is] acting" as a
prophet cannot be ascertained by the standard works. These strikes
against this teaching would seem to invalidate it according to Robinson's own rules.

Dr. Robinson's quote draws another question. If a membership
vote is required to make a doctrine binding, why were the major
changes that were made to the temple endowment ceremony in April
1990 not voted upon? And why wasn't the membership allowed to
vote on the changes made to the *Book of Mormon* in 1981? There is
no record of the membership being asked about such decisions.

According to the book *Gospel Principles*, Mormons are told they
can know precisely when their prophet is acting in the capacity of a
prophet:

> In addition to these four books of scripture, the inspired words
> of our living prophets become scripture to us. Their words come to
> us through conferences, Church publications, and instructions to
> local priesthood leaders.[12]

The above statement, taken from an LDS Church publication,
would seem to justify many of the teachings of past leaders that have
embarrassed current members. Many of the questionable doctrines
proposed by Mormon prophets have come from the tabernacle pulpit
at the biannual general conferences.

Although it is simple enough to discount past teachings of leaders
who are long dead, these men were just as serious about these teachings as current LDS leaders are about the doctrines that they propose

---

[11]*Documentary History of the Church* 5:265.
[12]*Gospel Principles*, pp. 51–52.

today. Brigham Young understood the importance of his position when he said in 1867:

> What man or woman on the earth, what spirit in the spirit-world can say truthfully that I ever gave a wrong word of counsel, or a word of advice that could not be sanctioned by the heavens? . . . I say this that you may understand that I feel just as patient, and just as kind toward the Latter-day Saints as a man's heart can feel, and am careful to take every precaution in directing their steps to the possession of eternal life in the presence of God that none may be lost.[13]

Was Brigham Young being flippant when he said he never gave wrong counsel or advice? If so, why trust him at all?

While many Latter-day Saints may find security in trusting only the standard works, they still must deal with the fact that their prophets also carry a great deal of authority.

The Standard Works Plus Prophets

Mormon Apostle James Talmage wrote:

> We believe that God is as willing today as He ever has been to reveal His mind and will to man, and that He does so through His appointed servants—prophets, seers, and revelators—invested through ordination with the authority of the Holy Priesthood. We rely therefore on the teachings of the living oracles of God as of equal validity with the doctrines of the written word.[14]

If the words of the prophet are of equal validity to the written word, Mormons cannot be so quick to distance themselves from past teachings. If both are inspired, there should be no contradiction.

Thirteenth LDS President Ezra Taft Benson saw no problem with contradictions between Mormon prophets and the standard works or even contradictions between Mormon prophets. In his *Fourteen Fundamentals in Following the Prophets* speech given on February 26, 1980, he justified the disparities by saying that the current living prophet is more vital to Latter-day Saints than the standard works

---

[13]*Journal of Discourses* 12:127–128.
[14]James E. Talmage, *The Articles of Faith*, 1982 ed., p. 7.

and warned his listeners not to "pit the dead prophets against the living prophets."[15]

In his speech, Benson related a story told by fourth President Wilford Woodruff during a church conference in 1897:

> I will refer to a certain meeting I attended in the town of Kirtland in my early days. At that meeting some remarks were made that have been made here today, with regard to the living oracles and with regard to the written word of God. The same principle was presented, although not as extensively as it has been here, when a leading man in the Church got up and talked upon the subject, and said: "You have got the word of God before you here in the Bible, the Book of Mormon, and Doctrines and Covenants; you have the written word of God, and you who give revelations should give revelations according to those books, as what is written in those books is the word of God. We should confine ourselves to them."
>
> When he concluded, Brother Joseph turned to Brother Brigham Young and said, "Brother Brigham I want you to take the stand and tell us your views with regard to the living oracles and the written word of God." Brother Brigham took the stand, and he took the Bible, and laid it down; he took the Book of Mormon, and laid it down; and he took the Book of Doctrine and Covenants, and laid it down before him, and he said: "There is the written word of God to us, concerning the work of God from the beginning of the world, almost, to our day. And now," said he, "when compared with the living oracles those books are nothing to me; those books do not convey the word of God direct to us now, as do the words of a Prophet or a man bearing the Holy Priesthood in our day and generation. I would rather have the living oracles than all the writing in the books." That was the course he pursued. When he was through, Brother Joseph said to the congregation; "Brother Brigham has told you the word of the Lord, and he has told you the truth."[16]

Benson must have really believed this account since he also told the story in a 1963 church conference.[17] The aforementioned narrative

---

[15]Benson, *Fourteen Fundamentals in Following the Prophets*, p. 4.
[16]Ibid., pp. 3, 4.
[17]*Conference Report*, October 1963, p. 17.

carries more weight than an average Mormon might think. It is important to note that there are four LDS presidents who agreed that the standard works do not have the highest priority when it comes to truth. Brigham Young gave the illustration to this effect, Joseph Smith agreed with it, and both Wilford Woodruff and Ezra Taft Benson related the story as a truism.

If "truth" can change with the induction of a new Mormon prophet, then Mormons really are doing nothing more than trusting in a mere mortal man. This is exactly what God, through the prophet Jeremiah, warned us not to do![18]

The scribes and Pharisees during Jesus' day added to the Word of God and bound the people with heavy burdens above and beyond those precepts found in the Scriptures. Today's Mormon leaders are really nothing less than Latter-day Pharisees who demand an impossible lifestyle of their people. Instead of experiencing the peace which passes all understanding,[19] many Mormons feel the pressure of anxiety and guilt.

As it turns out, many Mormons are not quite sure how they are supposed to sort out their theology. If the standard works are to be accepted as true, what about continuing revelation when a prophet contradicts it? If prophets speak with authority at conferences, why are Mormons told to ignore many of the teachings by past leaders that were mentioned during conferences?

The Journal of Discourses

Although the *Journal of Discourses* is a collection of sermons of various nineteenth-century Mormon leaders, Latter-day Saints are told to approach these volumes with caution. A common reason many Mormons give for not accepting the *Journal* is that they were poorly transcribed.

> Though the First Presidency endorsed the publication of the *Journal*, there was no endorsement as to the accuracy or reliability of the contents. There were occasions when the accuracy was questionable.[20]

---

[18]Jeremiah 17:5 reads, "Thus saith the Lord; Cursed be the man that trusteth in man, and maketh flesh his arm."
[19]Philippians 4:7.
[20]Gerald E. Jones, *A Sure Foundation*, p. 200.

PREFACE.

The *Journal of Discourses* deservedly ranks as one of the standard works of the Church, and every rightminded Saint will certainly welcome with joy every Number as it comes forth from the press as an additional reflector of " the light that shines from Zion's hill."

We rejoice, therefore, in being able to present to the Saints another completed Volume—the Eighth of the series; and, in doing so, we sincerely commend the varied and important instructions it contains to their earnest consideration.

THE PUDLISHRR.

Preface to Volume Eight of the *Journal of Discourses* states the journal ranks as a "standard work of the Church."

If the above statement is true, the LDS Church needs to explain why it includes so many quotes from the *Journal of Discourses* in its manuals. If they are not trustworthy, why does the LDS Church often refer to them? It is apparent that it is Mormonism's theological evolution and not the *Journal's* inaccuracy that drives LDS Church leaders to downplay their significance. Mormon doctrine has changed drastically since the times of Joseph Smith, Brigham Young, and John Taylor. The *Journal of Discourses* exposes this deviation since it is one set of books that the LDS Church has not doctored up.

The *Journal of Discourses* was published by George D. Watt with the blessing of Brigham Young. There is no reason to believe that Watt was not a faithful Mormon who did not love his church. To the contrary, Watt wanted his fellow Latter-day Saints to possess "the words of the Apostles and Prophets, as they were spoken in the Assemblies of the Saints in Zion." Watt claimed the *Journal* contained "purity of doctrine, simplicity of style, and an extensive amount of theological truth." He even went on to say that the sermons he recorded would prove to be a source of light to those who sincerely desired to know the truth.[21]

Certainly Mormon Apostle John Widtsoe did not think the *Journal of Discourses* was based on inferior transcriptions since he used Watt's recordings to produce his book entitled *The Discourses of Brigham Young*. In the preface, Widtsoe wrote:

> This book was made possible because Brigham Young secured stenographic reports of his addresses. As he traveled among the people, reporters accompanied him. All that he said was recorded. Practically all these discourses (from December 16, 1851 to August 19, 1877) were published in the *Journal of Discourses*, which was widely distributed. The public utterances of a few great historical figures have been so faithfully and fully preserved. . . . The corrections for the printer, as shown by existing manuscripts, were few and of minor consequence.

President Woodruff vouched for the accuracy of the *Journal of Discourses* when he said:

> Sermons reported by G. D. Watts, one of the official reporters,

---

[21]Preface to *Journal of Discourses*, volume 1.

were considered as reported correctly, and they are found in the *Journal of Discourses*; they are considered correct. Some of my own sermons are published there, and they are correct.[22]

If the *Journal of Discourses* is inaccurate, why would an editorial in the Mormon publication *Millennial Star* urge readers to secure a set? The set was enthusiastically endorsed:

> It would be well if all our readers would secure a copy of the Journal of Discourses as it is issued, and also every standard work of the Church; and not only secure these works but attentively read them and thoroughly study the principles they contain.[23]

In a letter dated June 12, 1963, Axel J. Andreasen, assistant manager of Deseret Book Company, said:

> In having in your library the twenty-six volumes of the "Journals of Discourses," you have a library containing the sermons of the Presidents and Apostles of the Church. If anyone tells you that the sermons found therein are not recognized by the Church, they know not what they are talking about. I am sure that the individual is not anyone in authority—certainly not among the General Authorities. It could be a stake authority or a ward authority, but the opinion that the individual has expressed to you is absolutely erroneous.[24]

In the above letter, Mr. Andreasen notes that the title pages in the *Journal of Discourses* state the volumes were published in London at the LDS printing office where "all of the church publications were printed in England in the early days of the opening of the British Mission." Why would the LDS Church print the *Journal* if these volumes do not reflect Mormon teaching as it was at that time?

Since the accuracy of the *Journal* is an artificial excuse, it would seem to appear that the reason Mormons do not take the volumes seriously is because they expose the heretical teachings of past leaders. Mormons who have read and downplay the *Journal of Discourses* know these aberrational teachings undermine the authority and claims of the LDS Church.

---

[22]Woodruff, *Temple Lot Case Testimony*, p. 309, 1893.
[23]*Millennial Star* 15:780.
[24]Letter to Mr. H. C. Combes, June 12, 1963.

It is irrelevant to say these teachings should not be given serious consideration because they are not in the standard works. Were these leaders teaching truth when they spoke or weren't they? If they were, what does it matter if it is not in the standard works? If they were not teaching truth, why should members be compelled to honor them as godly spiritual guides?

What If the Bible Is Translated Correctly After All?

The eighth of Mormonism's Thirteen Articles of Faith found at the end of the *Pearl of Great Price* says, "We believe the Bible to be the Word of God as far as it is translated correctly; we also believe the *Book of Mormon* to be the word of God."

In other words, Mormons are taught to accept the King James Version of the Holy Bible except in those areas where they say it is translated incorrectly. When trying to witness to a Mormon by using the Bible, you may be told that the verses which you quote are flawed. The *Book of Mormon*, on the other hand, is given full status in the eighth Article of Faith as being the "word of God" without any qualifying statements!

Robert J. Matthews, a dean of religious education at Brigham Young University, says that many biblical errors were corrected in other LDS standard works. He writes:

> Many important concepts once in the Bible but now missing from it have been restored through the Book of Mormon and other Latter-day revelations.[1]

---

[1]*A Sure Foundation*, p. 165.

THE BIBLE ALONE AN INSUFFICIENT GUIDE.

much money to furnish himself with manuscripts : yet, in conclusion, he was forced to desist utterly, lest, if he should ingeniously have noted all the several differences of reading which himself had collected, the incredible multitude of them almost in every verse, should rather have made men atheistical, than satisfy them in the true reading of any particular passage."* Let those who take the Bible for their only guide think of this. If the few manuscripts procured by Bishop Usher, contains in almost every verse " *an incredible multitude of different readings,*" what grounds have Protestants for confidence in one of these readings more than in another ? Out of a thousand different manuscripts, differing in almost every text, who can select the true one ? Indeed, there would be almost an infinite improbability as to any one copy being true. Now, it was from such a mass of contradictory Greek manuscripts that the English New Testament was translated.

47.—But to say nothing of the incredible multitude of different readings in the Greek manuscripts themselves, the translators from these old manuscripts are liable to commit many errors, as is evident from the vast number of very different translations which have been made. There is no two translations that agree. This then is another prolific source of error which is calculated to throw still greater uncertainty over the present copies of the scriptures.

48.—What shall we say then, concerning the Bible's being a sufficient guide ? Can we rely upon it in its present known corrupted state, as being a faithful record of God's word ? We all know that but a few of the inspired writings have descended to our times, which few quote the names of some twenty other books which are lost, and it is quite certain that there were many other inspired books that even the names have not reached us.† What few have come down to our day, have been mutilated, changed, and corrupted, in such a shameful manner that no two manuscripts agree. Verses and even whole chapters have been added by unknown persons ; and even we do not know the authors of some whole books ; and we are not certain that all those which we do know, were wrote by inspiration. Add all this imperfection to the uncertainty of the translation, and who, in his right mind, could, for one moment, suppose the Bible in its present form to be a perfect guide ? Who knows that even one verse of the whole Bible has escaped pollution, so as to convey the same sense now that it did in the original ? Who knows how many important doctrines and ordinances necessary to salvation may be buried in oblivion in some of the lost books ? Who knows that even the ordinances and doctrine that seem to be set forth in the present English Bible, are anything like the original ? The Catholics and Protestants do not know, because tradition is too imperfect to give this knowledge. There can be no certainty as to the contents of the inspired writings until God shall inspire some one to re-write all those books over again, as he did Esdras in ancient times. There is no possible means of arriving at certainty in any other way. No reflecting man can deny the necessity of such a new revelation.

49.—We now appeal to the honesty, good sense, and learning of all good moral men, to testify their convictions in regard to the insufficiency of their rules of faith. Is there a man among you who has candidly examined the present confused, divided, distracted state of all Christendom, who is not thoroughly convinced that something is radically wrong ? Many of you, no doubt, have, in your serious reflecting moments, looked upon the bewildered, blind, cold, formal, powerless systems of religion with which you were surrounded with feelings of sorrow and disgust. You have wished to know the truth, but alas, wherever you have turned your investigations, darkness and uncertainty have stared you in the face. The voices of several hundred jarring, contending, soul-sickening sects, were constantly sounding in your ears ; each one professing to be built upon the Bible, and yet each one differing from all the rest. Under this confused state of things, you have peradventure, involuntarily exclaimed ; can the Bible be the word of God ! Would God reveal a system of religion expressed in such *indefinite terms* that a thousand different religions should grow out of it ? Has God revealed the great system of salvation in such vague uncertain language on purpose to delight himself with the quarrels and contentions of his creatures in relation

* Exomol. Ca. 8. Nu. 3.
† Esdras speaks of a great number of books which we have not got.

Mormon Apostle Orson Pratt implies that none of the Bible can be trusted. (*Divine Authenticity of the Book of Mormon,* p. 47.)

Bear in mind, Mr. Matthews' statement is based purely on subjective reasoning and cannot be supported by either historical or textual evidence. The Mormon Church claims that many books of the Bible have been lost. It does not include any of these so-called lost books in its standard works.

Since Mormonism's beginning, the Bible has been viewed with suspicion. Joseph Smith exclaimed:

> Ignorant translators, careless transcribers, or designing and corrupt priests have committed many errors.[2]

An account in the *Book of Mormon* allegedly translated by Smith, mocks the use of the Bible as a lone scriptural guide when it says:

> And because my words shall hiss forth—many of the Gentiles shall say: A Bible! A Bible! We have got a Bible, and there cannot be any more Bible.[3]

Early Mormon Apostle Orson Pratt believed that the Bible was marred and could not be trusted. He wrote:

> . . . who, in his right mind, could, for one moment, suppose the Bible in its present form to be a perfect guide? Who knows that even one verse of the Bible has escaped pollution?[4]

Mormon Apostle Mark E. Petersen further disparaged the Bible when he wrote:

> Many insertions were made, some of them 'slanted' for selfish purposes, while at times deliberate falsifications and fabrications were perpetrated.[5]

With statements like these, no wonder the Mormon people do not have complete faith in the Bible! Contrary to the misinformation many Mormons are given concerning the Bible, there is plenty of proof to demonstrate that it is a reliable source for truth.

In *Evidence That Demands a Verdict*, Christian apologist/evangelist Josh McDowell spends the first quarter of his book defending the reliability of the Bible. Among his many excellent points, McDowell

---

[2]Joseph Fielding Smith, editor, *Teachings of the Prophet Joseph Smith*, p. 327.
[3]2 Nephi 29:3.
[4]Pratt, *Divine Authenticity of the Book of Mormon*, p. 47.
[5]Mark E. Petersen, *As Translated Correctly*, p. 4.

notes the uniqueness of the Bible. The Bible is actually a compilation of many books (66 to be exact) written by more than 40 authors over a 1,500-year time span. Parts of the Bible were written on three different continents in three languages (Hebrew, Aramaic, and Greek) . . . yet it is in complete agreement with itself.[6]

Regarding the prophecies included within the Bible, Christian scholar Charles Ryrie noted:

> Could these predictions have happened by chance? If so, then they would not validate the Bible. If, however, they could not possibly happen by chance, then we ought to take notice of what the Bible says in other matters, since it has proved itself to be reliable in the testable area of fulfilled prophecies. . . . There are more than 30 predictions about the life of Jesus. In addition, there are many other prophecies recorded in the Bible that have already been fulfilled. The total number is certainly more than 100. The probability of 100 prophecies being fulfilled by chance is less than one in 1,000,000,000,000,000,000,000,000,000,000.[7]

Compared to other ancient writings, the Bible is extremely reliable. Take the New Testament, for example.

> There are now more than 5,300 known Greek manuscripts of the New Testament. Add over 10,000 Latin Vulgate and at least 9,300 other early versions (MSS) and we have more than 24,000 manuscript copies of portions of the New Testament in existence today. No other document of antiquity even begins to approach such numbers and attestation. In comparison, the Iliad by Homer is second with only 643 manuscripts that still survive. The first complete preserved text of Homer dates from the thirteenth century.[8]

On the other hand, the original books found in the New Testament were written between A.D. 40–100. The earliest manuscript in existence is the John Rylands Manuscript, which has been dated A.D. 130 and contains the book of John. Other important early manu-

---

[6] Josh McDowell, *Evidence That Demands a Verdict*, p. 16.
[7] Charles Ryrie, *Does It Really Matter What You Believe?*, p. 7.
[8] McDowell, *Evidence That Demands a Verdict*, p. 39. Bear in mind Homer lived only as far back as the eighth century B.C., while the Bible dates back much further than that.

scripts include the Bodmer Papyrus II (A.D. 150–200) and the Chester Beatty Papyri (A.D. 200). Nearly complete manuscripts, which are deemed most reliable by many scholars, can be traced back to no later than A.D. 400.

Christian scholar Sir Frederick Kenyon notes that the age of a manuscript really plays no part since new copies were deemed just as equal in authority as older copies:

> When a manuscript had been copied with the exactitude prescribed in the Talmud, and had been duly verified, it was accepted as authentic and regarded as being of equal value with any other copy. If all were equally correct, age gave no advantage to a manuscript; on the contrary, age was a positive disadvantage, since the manuscript was liable to become defaced or damaged in the lapse of time. A damaged or imperfect copy was at once condemned as unfit for use.[9]

It is true that there are textual differences between the manuscripts. However, these manuscripts have been deciphered for accuracy and carefully compared to form the most accurate Greek text. Dr. Norman Geisler and William Nix say:

> Only about one-eighth of all the variants had any weight, as most of them are merely mechanical matters such as spelling or style. Of the whole, then, only about one-sixtieth rise above 'trivialities,' or can in any sense be called 'substantial variations.' Mathematically this would compute to a text that is 98.33 percent pure.[10]

As for the reliability of the Old Testament, Dr. Gleason Archer writes:

> A careful study of the variants (different readings) of the various earliest manuscripts reveals that none of them affects a single doctrine of Scripture. The system of spiritual truth contained in the standard Hebrew text of the Old Testament is not in the slightest altered or compromised by any of the variant readings found in the Hebrew manuscripts. . . . It is very evident that the vast majority

[9]Sir Frederick Kenyon, *Our Bible and the Ancient Manuscripts*, 1941, p. 43.
[10]Dr. Norman Geisler and William Nix, *A General Introduction to the Bible*, p. 365.

of them are so inconsequential as to leave the meaning of each clause doctrinally unaffected.[11]

Kenyon concurred when he wrote that none of the so-called disputed readings affect in any way the tenets of the Christian faith.

> No fundamental doctrine of the Christian faith rests on a disputed reading. . . . It cannot be too strongly asserted that in substance the text of the Bible is certain: Especially is this the case with the New Testament.[12]

The 1947 discovery of the Dead Sea Scrolls, a group of manuscripts discovered in Qumran, Israel, which included most Old Testament writings and a number of commentaries produced between 200 B.C and 100 A.D., proves the accuracy of the Old Testament. Many zealous Latter-day Saints expected the scrolls to restore the lost truths expunged by "unscrupulous Bible translators" and, in turn, vindicate the *Book of Mormon* as a truly ancient document. This has not been the case. In fact, a BYU professor, Dr. Stephen E. Robinson, has said:

> So far, the plain and precious things have not been restored to us in the Dead Sea Scrolls. If Latter-day Saints would just get a good English translation of all the [already] published scrolls, they would discover that the people of Qumran are not [Latter-day] Saints of former days.[13]

Instead, the scrolls found in Qumran have further corroborated the Bible. One example of the importance of this discovery is a scroll which contained Isaiah 53. The earliest copy of Isaiah before the Dead Sea Scrolls was from the tenth century, bridging the gap by a millennium. Write Geisler and Nix:

> Of the 166 words in Isaiah 53, there are only seventeen letters in question. Ten of these letters are simply a matter of spelling, which does not affect the sense. Four more letters are minor stylistic changes, such as conjunctions. The remaining three letters comprise the word 'light,' which is added in verse 11, and does not affect the meaning greatly. Furthermore, this word is supported by

---

[11]Gleason Archer, *A Survey of the Old Testament*, p. 25.

[12]Kenyon, *Our Bible and the Ancient Manuscripts*, 1941, p. 23.

[13]*The Salt Lake Tribune*, "LDS Scholars Renew Interest in Mysterious Dead Sea Scrolls," December 7, 1991, A-5.

the LXX and IQ Is. Thus, in one chapter of 166 words, there is only one word (three letters) in question after a thousand years of transmission—and this does not significantly change the meaning of the passage.[14]

The information provided here is just a taste of what is available for a person who truly wants the facts concerning the reliability of the Bible. Unfortunately, most Mormons merely parrot other uninformed Mormons when it comes to the reliability of the Scriptures. While many Latter-day Saints proudly point to comments made by Pratt, McConkie, Petersen, and Matthews, etc., none of these men are/were experts in the field of biblical textual criticism.

When a Mormon does seriously examine the reliability of the ancient manuscripts, a different conclusion is drawn. For instance, BYU professor Richard L. Anderson's study of textual criticism has yielded just the opposite result. Speaking of the New Testament, Dr. Anderson remarked:

> For a book to undergo progressive uncovering of its manuscript history and come out with so little debatable in its text is a great tribute to its essential authenticity. First, no new manuscript discovery has produced serious differences in the essential story. This survey has disclosed the leading textual controversies, and together they would be well within one percent of the text. Stated differently, all manuscripts agree on the essential correctness of 99 percent of all the verses in the New Testament.[15]

A final note is that many Mormons are confused about the number of English Bible translations. It is true that there are dozens of Bible versions. Mormon writer James A. Carver concluded:

> Both Latter-day Saints and other Christians accept the Bible as God's word but the LDS are often criticized for adding the phrase, 'as far as it is translated correctly.' That shouldn't bother Christians too much since much of their time is spent in producing new translations. I have one Bible with eight translations and another one with twenty-six, which indicates that Christians, as well as

---

[14]Geisler and Nix, *A General Introduction to the Bible*, p. 263.
[15]Fourteenth Annual Symposium of the Archaeology of the Scriptures, Brigham Young University, 1963.

Latter-day Saints have some concerns about translation.[16]

While Carver's statement tries to question the accuracy of the Bible, he inadvertently raises the question regarding the accuracy regarding various translations of the *Book of Mormon*. The *1993–1994 Church Almanac* does not hide the fact that many editions of the *Book of Mormon* have been revised.[17] Because the LDS Church made substantial corrections to its English edition in the early 1980s, it would seem necessary that it will have to revise all of its foreign translations of the *Book of Mormon* in order for all editions to say the same thing.

Not even all of the splinter groups of Latter-day Saints would agree as to which *Book of Mormon* is the most correct; for instance, the *Book of Mormon* produced by the Reorganized Church of Jesus Christ of Latter Day Saints (RLDS) does not read exactly the same as the LDS edition. Which edition, the RLDS or LDS translation, was translated by the gift and power of God?

It is also important to realize that the Bible was written in Hebrew, Aramaic, and Greek. Therefore, there can be no "exact" translation to English just as there cannot be an "exact" translation between French and German or Spanish and Russian. Because each dialect is unique, there are many words and phrases within each language that cannot be adequately translated into other languages.

It is also a fact that the English language changes. Thus, while many Christians still use the King James Version published in the seventeenth century, its terminology and grammatical usage is much different from the twentieth century. Since many Christians (especially the younger believers) may have difficulty understanding older translations, godly men have produced a number of these contemporary English versions. Some are good and some are not so good. A good translation will remain as close as possible to the original languages while utilizing a contemporary, easy-to-understand vernacular. For those passages that remain confusing, a return to the original languages will usually clear up the matter. Many of the so-called "contradictions" can be clarified this way.

Unless a Mormon understands that the Bible alone is the Word of

---

[16]James A. Carver, *Answering an Ex-Mormon Critic*, p. 7.
[17]pp. 401–402. For instance, the German, Italian, Turkish, Japanese, and Armenian-Western editions are all listed as having been retranslated.

God, confusion on important matters of doctrine will continue to reign. As Timothy was told by Paul to "study to shew thyself approved unto God, a workman that needeth not to be ashamed, rightly dividing the word of truth,"[18] so should we discern truth via the Word of God, the Bible.[19]

---

[18]2 Timothy 2:15.
[19]For more information on this subject, see Chapter 13 in *Answering Mormons' Questions*, Bethany House Publishers, 1991.

FIVE

If the Bible Is Corrupt, Why Doesn't the LDS Church Use the Joseph Smith Translation of the Bible?

The *Inspired Version* of the Bible, also known as *The Joseph Smith Translation (JST)*, is a Bible version put together by Mormonism's founder, Joseph Smith. He believed that the Bible contained many errors that needed to be corrected, so, as God's prophet, he produced his own version. Today this translation is distributed by Herald House Publishers, which is owned by the Reorganized Church of Jesus Christ of Latter Day Saints (RLDS).

LDS scholars feel Smith probably began his translation as early as June 1830. A statement made by Smith in the *Times and Seasons* shows he began no later than December of 1830. It reads:

> It may be well to observe here, that the Lord greatly encouraged
> and strengthened the faith of his little flock, which had embraced
> the fulness of the everlasting gospel, as revealed to them in the
> Book of Mormon, by giving some more extended information upon
> the scriptures, a translation of which had already commenced.[1]

---

[1] *Times and Seasons* 4:336. Though this edition was printed in 1843, the statement mentioned above is taken from an article entitled *The History of Joseph Smith*, an ongoing article that appeared in a number of editions of the *Times and Seasons*. Page 320 of this volume places this event in December of 1830.

Technically, it is incorrect to say that the *JST* is a translation. Although Smith said God called it a "translation," Mormon Apostle John Widtsoe recognized this was misleading:

> It is not really correct to say that the Prophet translated the Bible. Rather, he corrected errors in the Bible, and under revelation added long statements.[2]

Mormon Apostle Bruce McConkie describes Joseph Smith's method of "translation" in the following manner:

> In consequence, at the command of the Lord and while acting under the spirit of revelation, the Prophet corrected, revised, altered, added to, and deleted from the King James Version of the Bible to form what is now commonly referred to as the *Inspired Version of the Bible*.[3]

Instead of diligently examining ancient texts, Smith was moved by nothing more than alleged inspiration:

> The "revision" or "translation" was done under a high degree of spiritual illumination. No reference books were used. No ancient documents were involved. There was no "Urim and Thummim."[4]

This source goes on to further say:

> No changes were made in Esther, Ecclesiastes, Lamentations, Obadiah, Micah, Nahum, Habakkuk, Zephaniah, Haggai, Malachi, or the Second and Third Epistles of John. This was because the manuscript noted all but Ecclesiastes as "correct." No comment occurs in relation to Ecclesiastes; for this reason it is included in the authorized version without change.[5]

It is interesting to note that Smith marked the book of Malachi "correct" since he specifically noted that the angel Moroni quoted it differently when he appeared to him in 1823.[6] Is the version as recorded in the *Inspired Version* or Moroni's account the correct translation of Malachi?

---

[2] Widtsoe, *Evidences and Reconciliations*, pp. 353–354.
[3] McConkie, *Mormon Doctrine*, p. 383, (emphasis his).
[4] *Joseph Smith's 'New Translation' of the Bible*, p. 18.
[5] Ibid., p. 16.
[6] *Joseph Smith History* 1:36–39.

Calling the *JST* a vast work, Mormon Apostle John Widtsoe stated:

> Drs. Sidney B. Sperry and Merrill Y. Van Wagoner state that 12,650 words were added in Genesis, and that 693 verses were changed in the other books of the Old Testament. In the New Testament, these authors say that 1,453 verses were changed. In the four gospels alone, 1,036 verses were altered. Certainly the Prophet used great effort to restore the original meaning of the Bible.[7]

Widtsoe boasts that this translation shows

> . . . the great service the Prophet Joseph Smith rendered in correcting Biblical errors, and to make the statements of the Holy Scriptures more understandable to the human mind. The "inspired translation" is one of the mighty evidences of the prophetic power of Joseph Smith.[8]

At a 1985 symposium held at Brigham Young University, BYU professor Robert J. Matthews said the *JST* is accurate when compared to Joseph Smith's own manuscript. According to Matthews, the *JST* contains many truths that are only hinted at in other translations:

> Why aren't these things in the Bibles the world has? I cannot believe that the ancient prophets and Apostles didn't have a clear understanding of the gospel, or that they didn't tell it. What I do believe is that all the writings as found in all known, ancient manuscripts have been altered and diluted so that what presently is regarded as their writings no longer contain many of the plain and precious and more particular parts of the gospel that once were there. . . . Much of this has been restored now through the Joseph Smith Translation.[9]

In his devotion to Joseph Smith, Matthews and others of like persuasion fail to accept that it could be Joseph Smith who did the altering and diluting. While many Mormons see no problem in questioning the ability of non-Mormon scholars, Joseph Smith is off limits to criticism!

According to the *Doctrine and Covenants*, God supposedly told Smith to not only translate a new Bible but also to finish it.

---

[7]Widtsoe, *Evidences and Reconciliations*, p. 354.
[8]Ibid., p. 356.
[9]*Ensign*, January 1985, p. 76.

And inasmuch as it is practicable, to preaching in the regions 'round about until conference; and after that it is expedient *to continue the work of translation until it be finished.*[10]

It would seem that Joseph Smith did finish this monumental task. In a letter dated July 2, 1833, he said:

We are exceedingly fatigued, owing to a great press of business. We this day finished the translating of the Scriptures, for which we returned gratitude to our Heavenly Father, and sat immediately down to answer your letters.[11]

The completion date of July 2, 1833 is also verified in Mormon historian Andrew Jensen's *Church Chronology* as well as the preface to the *Inspired Version.* Despite the references above, Mormons have been led to believe that their founder was not successful in fulfilling God's command. Men such as tenth LDS President Joseph Fielding Smith blamed this failure on interruptions caused by Joseph Smith's enemies:

The reason that it has not been published by the Church is due to the fact that this revision was not completed. . . . Due to persecution and mobbing this opportunity never came, so that the manuscript was left with only a partial revision.[12]

Scholars from both the LDS and RLDS camps cannot accept their founder's comment that he was finished with the translation because of the vast amount of inconsistencies it contains. Smith failed to change many parallel texts, which read the same in both Old and New Testaments.

Changes made at some points in the Inspired Version were not followed consistently. . . . Some passages were corrected, but the parallel references were not corrected. . . . Mormon authors Sperry and Van Wagoner have pointed out that the Psalms are evidence of the incompleteness of the translation.[13]

Rather than admit Smith's lack of inspiration, they are compelled

---

[10]*D & C* 73:4, (emphasis ours).
[11]*Documentary History of the Church* 1:368.
[12]Joseph Fielding Smith, *Answers to Gospel Questions* 2:207.
[13]*Joseph Smith's 'New Translation' of the Bible*, p. 11.

G. Williams were appointed and set apart by President Joseph Smith to be his Counselors in the Presidency of the Church, according to the revelation given March 8th. On the same occasion "many of the brethren saw a heavenly vision of the Savior and concourses of angels." (See History of Joseph Smith.)

Sat. 23.—A committee was appointed to purchase lands for the Saints at Kirtland.

Tues. 26.—An important council was held by the High Priests in Jackson County, Mo., in which some misunderstanding in regard to the presiding authorities in that land was amicably settled.

April.—In this month the first mob gathered at Independence, Jackson Co., Mo., to consult upon a plan for the removal or immediate destruction of the Church in that county.

Sat. 6.—About eighty official and some unofficial members of the Church met at the ferry on Big Blue river, near the western boundary of Jackson County, Mo., and, for the first time, celebrated the birthday of the Church.

May. Sat. 4.—Hyrum Smith, Jared Carter and Reynolds Cahoon were appointed a committee to obtain subscriptions for building a house for the Priesthood at Kirtland.

Mon. 6.—A revelation on the pre-existence of man was given through Joseph Smith, jun., at Kirtland, and on the same date the Saints were commanded by revelation to build a House to the Lord at Kirtland. (Doc. and Cov., Sec. 93 and 94.)

June. Sat. 1.—The Lord gave further instructions to Joseph the Prophet about the Temple to be built at Kirtland. (Doc. and Cov., Sec. 95.)

Tues. 4.—A revelation, showing the order of the Kirtland Stake of Zion, was given to Joseph Smith, jun. (Doc. and Cov., Sec. 96.)

Thurs. 6.—A conference of High Priests held at Kirtland, O., instructed the committee for building the House of the Lord to proceed at once in obtaining material for its construction.

Sun. 23.—Doctor P. Hurlburt, afterwards connected with the spurious Spaulding story, was excommunicated from the Church for adultery.

Tues. 25.—An explanation of the plat of the city of Zion was sent to the brethren in Jackson County, Mo. (See History of Joseph Smith.)

July.—By this time about twelve hundred Saints, including children, had gathered to Jackson County, Mo.

Tues. 2.—Joseph the Prophet finished the translation of the Bible.

Sat. 20.—The printing office belonging to the Saints at Independence, Jackson County, Mo., was destroyed by a mob, who also tarred and feathered Bishop Edward Partridge and a Brother Allen.

—Orson Pratt preached in Patten, Canada. This is supposed to be the first discourse preached by a Latter-day Saint Elder in The Dominion.

Tues. 23.—The Saints at Independence, Mo., made a treaty with the mob and consented to leave Jackson County. Oliver Cowdery was dispatched as a special messenger to Kirtland, O., to consult with the First Presidency.

—The corner stones of the Lord's House at Kirtland, O., were laid.

August. Fri. 2.—In a revelation given through Joseph Smith, jun., at Kirtland, the Lord commanded that a house be built to Him in the land of Zion by the tithing of His people. (Doc. and Cov., Sec. 97.)

Tues. 6.—The Saints were commanded by revelation to observe the constitutional laws of the land, to forgive their enemies and cultivate a spirit of charity toward all men. Their rights of self-defense were also made clear. (Doc. and Cov., Sec. 98.)

A few days later John Murdock was called to the ministry by revelation. (Doc. and Cov., Sec. 99.)

September. Wed. 11.—It was decided in council to establish a printing press at Kirtland, and publish a paper to be called the *Latter-day Saints' Messenger and Advocate;* also that the *Evening and Morning Star,* formerly published in Jackson County, Mo., should be published at Kirtland.

—Bishop Edward Partridge was acknowledged as the head of the Church in Zion, and ten High Priests were appointed to watch over the ten branches of the Church there.

October.—Orson Hyde and John Gould arrived in Jackson County, Mo., as messengers from Kirtland; and the Church in Zion dispatched Wm. W. Phelps and Orson Hyde to Governor Daniel Dunklin at Jefferson City, with a petition from the Saints.

Sat. 5.—Joseph Smith, jun., in company with Elders Sidney Rigdon and Freeman Nickerson, left Kirtland on a visit to Canada.

Tues. 8.—Wm. W. Phelps and Orson Hyde presented to Governor Daniel Dunklin, of Missouri, the petition from the Saints in Jackson County.

Sat. 12.—In a revelation given at Perrysburg, N. Y., Joseph Smith, jun., and Sidney Rigdon were commanded to continue their missionary labors in the East. (Doc. and Cov., Sec. 100.)

Sat. 19.—In answer to the petition from the Saints in Jackson County, Gov. Dunklin, of Missouri, wrote a letter to the leading men of the Church in that county, promising to enforce the laws.

Sat. 26.—Joseph Smith, jun., preached and baptized twelve persons at Mount Pleasant, Upper Canada.

Thurs. 31.—A mob attacked a branch of the Church, west of the Big Blue, in Jackson County, Mo., destroyed ten houses, and beat several of the brethren in a most brutal manner.

November. Fri. 1.—The Saints at Independence were attacked by a mob, and Gilbert & Whitney's store was partly destroyed, besides many private dwellings.

Sat. 2.—The mob attacked the Saints on the Big Blue, Jackson County, and beat David Bennett severely.

Mon. 4.—A skirmish took place between a company of Saints and a mob, several miles west of the Big Blue, in Jackson County. Andrew Barber, one of the Saints, was mortally wounded, two of the mob were killed, and several others wounded on both sides.

—Joseph Smith, jun., returned to Kirtland, O., from his mission to Canada.

LDS Church historian Andrew Jensen states that Joseph Smith's translation of the Bible was finished on July 2, 1833.

to say that he never really finished the job. If he didn't, this fails to explain why God would give the command to finish the translation when He knew it would not be fulfilled. God obviously expected Joseph Smith to finish this project because there are three references in the *Doctrine and Covenants* charging him to have it published. For instance, *D & C* 94:10 finds God commanding Smith to dedicate a lot for the building that would be used for the printing of Smith's Bible:

> And again, verily I say unto you, the second lot on the south shall be dedicated unto me for the building of a house unto me for the work of the printing of the translation of my scriptures, and all things whatsoever things I command you.[14]

The *Documentary History of the Church* has listed a number of books mentioned in the Bible that it does not contain.[15] Although there is no evidence to prove that these books were ever considered to be part of the canon, many Mormons still believe these are lost Scripture. Furthermore, with all the clamoring made by Mormon apologists over these books, you would think that God would have "inspired" Joseph Smith to reinsert them. If Smith's revision came by inspiration, why couldn't a restoration of "lost books" be performed the same way? Smith did not add these books to his version, but instead he excluded another one. Since Smith didn't think the Song of Solomon was inspired, he decided to leave it out.

Smith did not have to go far into the Bible to begin his rewrite. In Genesis 1:1, he began with the words, "And it came to pass," an expression found 1071 times throughout the *Book of Mormon*. Smith added twelve verses to the last chapter of Genesis, including a prophecy that "foretold" his own birth:

> And that seer will I bless, and they that seek to destroy him shall be confounded; for this promise I give unto you; for I will remember you from generation to generation; and his name shall be called Joseph, and it shall be after the name of his father; and he shall be like unto you; for the thing which the Lord shall bring forth by his hand shall bring my people salvation.[16]

---

[14]See also *D & C* 104:58; 124:89.
[15]*DHC* 1:132.
[16]Genesis 50:33, *JST*.

According to George A. Horton, Jr., an associate professor of Ancient Scripture at BYU,

> . . . reading Genesis without the benefit of the JST would be something like chewing on a T-bone with much of the steak already cut off.[17]

Smith would often correct the Bible while delivering sermons. This creates a problem because his corrections did not always concur with his 1833 translation. In 1844, while delivering his famous King Follett Discourse, Joseph Smith proclaimed:

> I have an old edition of the New Testament in the Hebrew, Latin, German, and Greek languages. I have been reading the German, and find it to be the most correct translation, and to correspond nearest to the revelations which God has given to me for the last fourteen years. It tells about Jachoboy, the son of Zebedee. It means Jacob. In the English New Testament it is translated James. Now, if Jacob had the keys, you might talk about James through all eternity, and never get the keys. In the 21st verse of the fourth chapter of Matthew, my old German edition gives the word Jacob instead of James.[18]

If Matthew 4:21 should really render the word Jacob for James, why didn't Joseph Smith correct it in his edition?[19] If God had been giving Smith revelations such as this for the past fourteen years, this would easily cover the time-period in which the *JST* was being done.

On June 16, 1844, Smith delivered a sermon dealing with the subject of a plurality of gods.

> President Joseph Smith read the 3rd chapter of Revelation, and took for his text 1st chapter, 6th verse—"And hath made us kings and priests unto God and His Father: to Him be glory and dominion forever and ever. Amen." It is altogether correct in the translation.[20]

There is little question that Smith attempted to use this verse to imply that the God of Mormonism had a Father. Bruce McConkie conceded this was true when he wrote:

---

[17]*Ensign*, January 1985, p. 77.
[18]*Journal of Discourses* 6:5.
[19]Matthew 4:21 in most Bibles is Matthew 4:20 in the *JST*.
[20]*Documentary History of the Church* 6:473.

The Prophet also taught—in explaining John's statement, "And hath made us kings and priests unto *God and his Father*" (Rev. 1:6)—That there is "a god above the Father of our Lord Jesus Christ. . . . *If Jesus Christ was the Son of God, and John discovered that God the Father of Jesus Christ had a Father, you may suppose that he had a Father also.*"[21]

Had Joseph Smith bothered to read the text from his *Inspired Version,* he could have never drawn such a conclusion. In rewriting this verse, he dropped the word "and" and inserts a comma: ". . . and hath made us kings and priests unto God, his Father."

In the same sermon mentioned above, Smith rendered a very loose recital of what appears to be Exodus 7:1. Stated Smith:

The scriptures are a mixture of very strange doctrines to the Christian world, who are blindly led by the blind. I will refer to another scripture. "Now," says God, when He visited Moses in the bush, (Moses was a stammering sort of a boy like me) God said, "Thou shalt be a God unto the children of Israel." God said, "Thou shalt be a God unto Aaron, and he shall be thy spokesman."[22]

The King James Version renders Exodus 7:1 as:

And the Lord said unto Moses, See, I have made thee a god to Pharaoh: and Aaron thy brother shall be thy prophet.[23]

This passage never says that Moses was to be a god unto the children of Israel or that Moses would be a god unto Aaron. In fact, Smith even removed any notion that Moses was a god to Pharaoh when he rewrote Exodus 7:1. The *JST* reads:

And the Lord said unto Moses, See, I have made thee a *prophet*

---

[21]McConkie, *Mormon Doctrine,* p. 577 (emphasis his).
[22]*Documentary History of the Church* 6:478.
[23]The phrase "make thee a god to Pharaoh" refers to the divine authority given to Moses. Many Bible texts such as the NKJV and NASB render this portion "make thee *as* god to Pharaoh." The NIV says, "make thee *like* god to Pharaoh." To imply this passage refers to deity would conflict with the many Bible verses that insist there exists only one God. To maintain that this refers to Moses' deity as Joseph Smith implied in his June 16, 1844 sermon, also conflicts with Mormon doctrine because Mormonism teaches Moses could not have reached godhood until after death, long after his confrontations with Pharaoh.

to Pharaoh, and Aaron thy brother shall be thy spokesman.[24]

If Joseph Smith really believed all along in a plurality of gods, why did he change verses in the Bible that could be interpreted (albeit incorrectly) to justify this teaching? Aside from the passages above, Smith also corrected Exodus 22:28. The King James Version reads:

Thou shalt not revile the gods, nor curse the ruler of thy people.

Smith changed this to read:

Thou shalt not revile against God, nor curse the ruler of thy people.

Joseph Smith also made a drastic change to John 1:1. Smith rendered this passage:

In the beginning was the gospel preached through the Son. And the gospel was the word, and the word was with the Son, and the Son was with God, and the Son was of God.

It is not uncommon for prevaricators to try to remove evidence that would expose their deceit. In Smith's case, it would be imperative that he doctor up any Bible verse that would conflict with his heretical views. Remember, he did not use any ancient texts to support his alterations. We have nothing to go by other than his capricious whims. For instance, to support his claim that he saw God, Smith altered John 1:18 to read, "And no man hath seen God at any time, *except he hath borne record of the Son.*"[25] He also altered 1 John 4:12 to read, "No man hath seen God at any time, *except them who believe. . . .*"[26]

Although the *JST* has never been published in whole by the LDS Church, it has sanctioned Smith's version by including his changes in both the footnotes and appendix of its official King James Version of the Bible. Some leaders have encouraged its use. Because the "Bible abounds in errors and mistranslations," Bruce McConkie advised Latter-day Saints to "use and rely on the Joseph Smith Translation."[27] McConkie believed "all necessary changes shall be made in the Bible,

---

[24]Emphasis ours.
[25]John 1:19 in the *JST* (emphasis ours).
[26]Emphasis ours.
[27]*Sunstone*, "Use 'Inspired Version,' Urges Apostle," 1985, 10:1, p. 47.

and the Inspired Version—as then perfected—shall go forth to the world."[28]

Should that day ever come, the Mormon Church will also have to revise the *Book of Mormon* again because entire chapters from the book of Isaiah are copied almost word for word from the King James Version, portions of which read differently from the *Inspired Version*.[29] Admittedly, most of these corrections involve only slight word changes, which do not change the meaning. While many Mormons criticize the many Bible translations, which use different words and sentence structures but convey the same message, they do not feel it is wrong for the *Inspired Version* to do the same thing.

If the Bible is as inaccurate as Mormon leaders have asserted, why haven't current LDS prophets corrected it? The *Doctrine and Covenants* does not deny this possibility when it says:

> And again, the duty of the President of the office of the High Priesthood is to preside over the whole church, and to be like unto Moses . . . to be a seer, a revelator, a *translator*, and a prophet, having all the gifts of God which he bestows upon the head of the church.[30]

Throughout history, the Bible has been highly regarded as Christianity's sacred Scriptures. Men and women of God have jeopardized their lives in order to defend and protect it. It seems strange that an organization that claims to be Christian with authority from God and whose current prophet is supposed to have the same power of translation as its founder would not rush to create an accurate version of the Bible. The fact that the LDS Church has wasted no time correcting the *Book of Mormon* over the years would demonstrate that a "correct" *Book of Mormon* carries a higher priority than a "correct" Bible.

---

[28]McConkie, *Mormon Doctrine*, p. 385.
[29]For example, compare 1 Nephi 21 with Isaiah 29; 2 Nephi 7 with Isaiah 50; and 2 Nephi 12–24 with Isaiah 2–14.
[30]*D & C* 107:91–92, (emphasis ours).

Why Should a Person Pray About the *Book of Mormon* When the Bible Says We Should Not Rely On Such a Subjective Test?

When sharing their faith, many Mormons (especially the LDS missionaries) will challenge potential converts to, first, read the *Book of Mormon* and, second, pray about its message to see if it is true. Mormons are taught that a "burning in the bosom," or good feelings, will occur if this test is taken. It is assumed that rational thought should be disregarded while this so-called spiritual test is applied.

A verse often cited is James 1:5. It says, "If any of you lack wisdom, let him ask of God, that giveth to all men liberally, and upbraideth not; and it shall be given him."

Another verse that is usually quoted comes from the *Book of Mormon* itself. Moroni 10:4 says:

> And when ye shall receive these things, I would exhort you that ye would ask God, the Eternal Father, in the name of Christ, if these things are not true; and if ye shall ask with a sincere heart, with real intent, having faith in Christ, he will manifest the truth of it unto you by the power of the Holy Ghost.

Another Mormon scripture promises:

> But, behold, I say unto you, that you must study it out in your

mind; then you must ask me if it be right, and if it is right I will cause that your bosom shall burn within you; therefore, you shall feel that it is right.[1]

Former Mormon Seventy John A. Widtsoe claimed that everyone who has searched for a Mormon testimony has found it. He wrote:

> Thousands have tried this approach to truth; and have found the testimonies they sought. So far, no one who, with flaming desire, sincere prayer, earnest study, and fearless practice, has sought the truth of "Mormonism" has failed to find it. Some, for lack of courage, though truth stared them in the face, have kept it to themselves. But, the approach never fails, so declares fearlessly the Church of Jesus Christ of Latter-day Saints.[2]

In fact, LDS Seventy Gene R. Cook believes this test will be successful "every time we wish to have eternal truth confirmed." Cook states, "When our asking has truly been an exercise in faith in Christ, we will be rewarded with an answer through the power of the Holy Ghost—but it will be according to the Lord's timing, not ours."[3]

The idea that feelings can substantiate truth does not end with a testimony. Rex Lee, president of the LDS Brigham Young University, believes that feelings can prove whether or not historical events took place. Regarding the bestowing of the Aaronic Priesthood upon Joseph Smith by John the Baptist and the Melchizedek Priesthood by Peter, James, and John, he explained:

> I not only believe, but know that it happened. No, I was not there in 1820 when Joseph Smith saw the Father and the Son. Neither was it my privilege to be present at the Susquehanna River in 1829. . . . Instead, I know through the power of the Holy Ghost, which the Lord has promised will teach the truth to his disciples and testify of him . . . so that not seeing, they may believe. . . . This testimony is available to all who enquire of God with honesty, desire, and faith.[4]

If a person were to follow this approach, a potentially good feeling

[1]*D & C* 9:8.
[2]Widtsoe, *Evidences and Reconciliations*, p. 17.
[3]*Ensign*, April 1994, pp. 12, 14.
[4]Lee, *What Do Mormons Believe?* p. 8.

one receives after praying about the truthfulness of a religion should take precedence over what is known to be true according to the Holy Bible. This is one reason why many Mormons refuse to listen to the facts, even when they are presented from the Bible. Feelings can, and often do, become more important than facts.

A common approach by the Latter-day Saints is to ask the skeptical non-Mormon if he or she has prayed about the *Book of Mormon*. If not, the skeptic is told to take the test through prayer. The Bible contains several powerful verses that tell the believer that prayer would not be the proper test in this area.

First John 4:1 says, "Beloved, believe not every spirit, *but try the spirits* whether they are of God: because many false prophets are gone out into the world."[5] A faith that cannot stand up to God's requirements should be rejected. First Thessalonians 5:21 adds, "Prove all things; hold fast that which is good." When two or more who had the gift of prophecy spoke at a gathering, Paul exhorted the Christians in 1 Corinthians 14:27–29 to have the people carefully judge the validity of the messages.

It is important to note that there is not a single statement made by any of the apostles that tells the potential convert to pray about the truthfulness of Christianity. Instead, the Old Testament Scriptures and the oral teachings of Jesus were quoted in an attempt to change the minds of the people. There was never an invitation to pray for a particular feeling.

The seventeenth chapter of Acts contains an excellent example proving this principle. When Paul preached in Berea, the people of the city did not accept his message merely because of the apostle's status. Rather, verse 11 says the Bereans "were more noble" than the Thessalonians because they accepted the Gospel message only after thoroughly searching the Scriptures to ascertain Paul's interpretation. In effect, they followed the pattern set by Christ who combatted Satan with Scripture during His temptation by Satan.[6]

Then, when Paul went to Athens, he reasoned with the Jews in the synagogues and those who met him in the marketplace. When he was brought to Mars Hill (a meeting place where religion and philos-

---

[5]Emphasis ours. The word "try" in Greek (dokimazo) literally means "to examine, prove or test."
[6]Matthew 4:1ff.

ophy were regular topics of discussion), Paul took a bold stand by using clear, logical thinking. His logic regarding the "unknown God" piqued the Athenians' interest and they asked him back to present further arguments.

If Paul were to agree with Mormon thought as presented in Moroni 10:4, this would have been a perfect opportunity to have appealed to prayer as being the solution to discover the validity of Christianity. He could have said, "Ye men of Athens, you too can receive a burning in the bosom and know that my religion is true if you would merely read the Scriptures and then pray about it." Yet he did not.

Concerning James 1:5 as referred to above by Rex Lee, there may be no other verse in the Bible that has been so poorly exegeted than the LDS interpretation. We do not know a single evangelical Christian commentator who suggests that this verse advocates praying about a religion to see if it might be true.

A prevailing view regarding James 1:5 is held by the highly regarded Reformation leader John Calvin. He felt verse five should be interpreted in light of verses two through four. That is, if a person is going through a trial, he or she should pray to God for wisdom regarding that trial. If this person should ask with honest intent, God will provide refuge via wisdom. This view seems to be most logical, especially considering how the following verses (12–17) expound on these trials and temptations. As in all cases, the context of any verse should always be dealt with before any interpretation is made.

There are other commentators who limit the connection between verses 2–4 and verse 5. However, while these scholars feel that James is making a general statement related to other scripture on wisdom,[7] it appears that only Mormon writers attempt to make this passage say that a religion should be chosen based on wisdom received through prayer.

Suppose a person does pray about the *Book of Mormon* and then claims that God told him it was a fictional tale, that Joseph Smith was a false prophet, and that Mormonism was false. Where should a person go from there? The obvious LDS counter to these statements is that, if you don't arrive at the right conclusion (that the *Book of Mormon* is true), you must not have had a sincere heart, real intent, or faith in Christ as required by Moroni 10:4. In other words, it's your

---

[7]i.e. Proverbs 8:35; 9:1–6; etc.

fault if you don't arrive at the desired LDS conclusion.

If James 1:5 does refer to praying about the validity of what Mormons call "another testament of Jesus Christ," then it would only be fair for the Mormon to accept other religious books as being true because the followers of those particular scriptures sincerely accept their religion's book(s) as coming from God. According to this logic, any book that produces a good feeling must be true. If subjectivity is a divinely ordained test for truth, then God could not in righteousness condemn anyone for a sincerely held belief. Obviously a more objective test must be implemented in order to determine truth.

It is unfortunate how most Mormons will often allow their feelings to control their thought processes. True Christians are not immune from this problem either. Mormons may suffer when dealing with an emotional problem such as depression when relying on their feelings to determine the veracity of their faith. "Does God still love me?" or "Am I still good enough for heaven?" are common questions that may plague an individual. Christians with a true belief in the Jesus of the Bible have been promised that "I will never leave you nor forsake you."[8]

One former Mormon apostle, George Q. Cannon, went so far as to say that the Spirit of God, which is received by a Mormon through prayer, should produce happy feelings; sad feelings can be attributed to Satan. In 1873, he wrote:

> I will tell you a rule by which you may know the Spirit of God from the spirit of evil. The Spirit of God always produces joy and satisfaction of mind. When you have the Spirit you are happy; when you have another spirit you are not happy. The spirit of doubt is the spirit of the evil one; it produces uneasiness and other feelings that interfere with happiness and peace."[9]

Feelings are not bad in and of themselves. When a person receives Jesus Christ as Lord and Savior, good feelings should follow. According to Christian author Peter H. Davids:

> Paul . . . argues that one knows if one is a Christian because of the presence of the Spirit within (Romans 8:9; see 1 John 3:24; 4:13). Acts also connects the reception of the Spirit to Christian

---

[8]Hebrews 13:5; Romans 8:31ff.
[9]*Journal of Discourses* 15:375–376.

initiation (2:38; 3:19; 8:15–17; 10:44–48; 19:5–6).[10]

John Wesley, the eighteenth-century Christian who wrote the hymns "Hark! the Herald Angels Sing" and "O for a Thousand Tongues," had a typical experience when he was invited to an evangelistic meeting in London. When he heard someone read from Luther's commentary on the Book of Romans, and the reader reached the description of the change that God works in the heart through faith in Christ, Wesley felt his heart "strangely warmed." He felt that he did trust in Christ alone for salvation; and had assurance that his sins had been taken away and he was saved from the law of sin and death.

Like Wesley, true Christians have a foundation that is stronger than their inner feelings. His name is Jesus Christ. It is impossible, however, to expect to feel good every minute of every day. Living produces problems. People die, disasters happen, and we as human beings (even Christians) were not meant to always feel good. The pressure to be happy in all situations is an impossible goal and will never be met. Even Jesus had emotions such as anger, sadness, and pain, both physical and emotional. It would be ludicrous to say that these feelings came from Satan.

Praying for a spiritual sensation is neither a biblical principle nor is it logically consistent. A person could pray as much as he wanted about defying gravity when jumping off a 50-story building. Yet no matter how confident a person believes that it is possible to safely land after such a jump, it is a fact that ten out of ten people who attempt this act without a bungee cord, parachute, or a special landing pad will be killed.

So it is with sincerity in religion. The Bible clearly shows that ten out of ten people who do not recognize the Jesus of the Bible as their Savior will die in their sins and be eternally damned.[11] "Happy feelings" or not, a person's sincerity cannot change that fact. Before change can occur in anybody's life, including a sincere Mormon, this truth needs to be conveyed and understood.

---

[10]Walter Kaiser, Jr., *More Hard Sayings of the New Testament*, p. 204.
[11]John 8:24.

Is It Wise to Place Blind Trust in Mere Mortal Men?

Mormon doctrine teaches that God reveals himself to the LDS prophet. This is integral to the claim that the LDS Church is the only true church. Mormonism's founder, Joseph Smith, stated that he restored the office of prophet to the world and proclaimed:

> God made Aaron to be the mouthpiece for the children of Israel, and He will make me be god to you in His stead, and the Elders to be mouth for me; and if you don't like it, you must lump it.[1]

Before he became the fourth LDS president, Wilford Woodruff said:

> Now, whatever I might have obtained in the shape of learning, by searching and study respecting the arts and sciences of men, whatever principles I may have imbibed during my scientific researches, yet, if the Prophet of God should tell me that a certain principle or theory which I might have learned was not true, I do not care what my ideas might have been, I should consider it my duty, at the suggestion of my file leader, to abandon that principle or theory. . . . It would be my duty to lay those principles aside,

---

[1]Joseph Fielding Smith, editor, *Teachings of the Prophet Joseph Smith*, p. 363.

and to take up those that might be laid down by the servants of God.[2]

Heber C. Kimball, a first counselor to Brigham Young who viewed Joseph Smith as a "dictator when it came to the things of God,"[3] added, "But if you are told by your leader to do a thing, do it. None of your business whether it is right or wrong."[4] Former Apostle George Q. Cannon agreed and said "opposing authority [is] a deadly sin."[5]

In a sermon given on January 29, 1860, Mormon Apostle Orson Pratt asked the question:

> Have we not a right to make up our minds in relation to the things recorded in the word of God, and speak about them, whether the living oracles believe our views or not? We have not the right. . . . God placed Joseph Smith at the head of this Church; God has likewise placed Brigham Young at the head of this Church; and he has required you and me, male and female, to sustain those authorities thus placed over us in their position. . . . We are commanded to give heed to their words in all things, and receive their words as from the mouth of God. . . . [6]

According to this rationale, the Mormon prophet is always right even if he is wrong. In 1970, eleventh LDS President Harold B. Lee said:

> Your safety and ours depends upon whether or not we follow the ones whom the Lord has placed to preside over his church. He knows whom he wants to preside over this church, and he will make no mistake. The Lord doesn't do things by accident. . . . Let's keep our eye on the President of the Church.[7]

Even individual thinking on the part of the Mormon is challenged. One LDS Church publication stated:

> Any Latter-day Saint who denounces or opposes, whether actively or otherwise, any plan or doctrine advocated by the prophets,

---

[2]*Journal of Discourses* 5:83.
[3]*Journal of Discourses* 2:106.
[4]*Journal of Discourses* 6:32.
[5]Cannon, *Gospel Truth*, p. 215.
[6]*Journal of Discourses* 7:374–375.
[7]Conference Report, October 1970, pp. 152–153, as quoted in *Living Prophets for a Living Church*, p. 32.

seers, and revelators of the Church is cultivating the spirit of apostasy. . . . It should be remembered that Lucifer has a very cunning way of convincing unsuspecting souls that the General Authorities of the Church are as likely to be wrong as they are to be right. This sort of game is Satan's favorite pastime, and he has practiced it on believing souls since Adam. He wins a great victory when he can get members of the Church to speak against their leaders and to "do their own thinking."[8]

To make sure the reader would understand what was just written, it added:

When our leaders speak, the thinking has been done. When they propose a plan—it is God's plan. When they point the way, there is no other which is safe. When they give direction, it should mark the end of controversy.[9]

The article's statement has never been officially refuted by LDS Church headquarters.

Another "obey at all cost" quote was made in 1979 by N. Eldon Tanner, the first counselor in the First Presidency, who responded to a statement made by Young Women General President Elaine Cannon at the October 1978 General Conference. Cannon had said:

Personal opinions may vary. Eternal principles never do. When the prophet speaks, sisters, the debate is over.[10]

Instead of criticizing this statement, which sounds very similar to the *Improvement Era* article, Tanner referred to Cannon's speech and said,

I was impressed by that simple statement, which carries such deep spiritual meaning for all of us. Wherever I go, my message to the people is: Follow the prophet. . . . When the prophet speaks, the debate is over.[11]

This thought is supported by LDS Apostle M. Russell Ballard when he said that "modern revelation to living prophets is just as profound

---

[8]*Improvement Era*, June 1945, p. 354.
[9]Ibid.
[10]*Ensign*, November 1978, p. 108.
[11]*Ensign*, August 1979, pp. 2–3.

as books of scripture." At an August 1991 fireside address given to Mormon missionaries, he taught:

> Do not take this fact casually that we have a living prophet and that we have living apostles on the face of the earth. Listen to what they teach. When general conference comes, pay attention to what they're saying. . . . Isn't it exciting to live in a time when we have a prophet of God to tell us what needs to be done.[12]

John A. Widtsoe, an earlier LDS apostle, taught that church doctrine should not be accepted blindly. He wrote:

> The doctrine of the Church cannot be fully understood unless it is tested by mind and feelings, by intellect and emotions, by every power of the investigator. Every Church member is expected to understand the doctrine of the Church intelligently. There is no place in the Church for blind adherence.[13]

Despite his quote, Widtsoe believed that true revelation only came through the Presidency with the prophet as the mediator between God and man. He wrote:

> If we need revelation for our guidance, what channel should they come through? The Lord will speak to us through the head of His Church, through him who holds the Presidency. . . . If any person other than the Presidency should profess to receive revelations for its government, would you consider them genuine revelations? If so, you would be mistaken.[14]

Ezra Taft Benson felt that the LDS prophet should always be obeyed. In a 1980 speech, he pointed out that the prophet speaks for God in everything and will never lead the LDS Church astray. He said that the prophet "is not required to have any particular earthly training or credentials" and can "speak on any subject or act on any matter at any time." Benson also taught that the prophet does not have to say "Thus saith the Lord" to give authoritative Scripture.[15]

While many Mormons will profess their loyalty to the Mormon prophet and believe he could supersede LDS scriptures, many in the

---

[12]*Church News*, August 10, 1991, p. 7.

[13]Widtsoe, *Evidences and Reconciliations*, p. 226.

[14]Widtsoe, *Priesthood and Church Government*, p. 248.

[15]Benson, *14 Fundamentals in Following the Prophets*, p. 3.

liberal Mormon community believe that limitations should be attached. If the prophet says something with which they disagree, liberal Mormons tend to classify it as mere opinion.

While this may sound logical, it contradicts the LDS leadership and, thus, Mormonism. If it is all right for a Mormon to arbitrarily override a teaching from the living prophet, there is no need to have a prophet in the first place. It is interesting to note that many Mormons do not agree with the prophet or with one another. There are different types of Mormons ranging from the liberal "Sunstone Mormon," who is less apt to believe the prophet, to conservative Mormons who toe the line and accept anything coming from the prophet's mouth to be scripture. It is dangerous to put so much trust in a single individual, especially when he could give doctrine that contradicts the Bible.

Should the LDS prophet be trusted when he is mentally incapacitated? This situation occurred in the early 1990s when Ezra Taft Benson, the thirteenth president, who was born in 1899, delegated his duties to other authorities. Those who were close to President Benson claimed that, while he was able to listen, he did not say very much and had "difficulty saying more than a few words."[16] Former Brigham Young University scholar and historian D. Michael Quinn said:

> When the Mormon prophet is mentally diminished, that is a personal tragedy. For these men to be stricken with mental confusion after a lifetime of dedication to the church is an existential crisis for believers like me. But institutionally it is a nightmare and can be a challenge to the faith of millions.[17]

Previous prophets with debilitating health include ninth President David O. McKay, who was ninety-six when he died. According to Quinn, McKay had a short-term memory loss who "would forget within minutes after a decision was made." Joseph Fielding Smith became the LDS president at ninety-three years of age and suffered from confusion and memory loss until he died several years later. In 1973, Spencer Kimball became the twelfth president at seventy-eight and was incapacitated mentally after a subdural hematoma in 1982.

---

[16]*Salt Lake Tribune*, January 16, 1993, Religion section, pp. C-1–C-2.
[17]Ibid.

He remained in this state until his death in 1985.[18]

The idea of an incoherent prophet who is supposed to be the direct link between man and God is offensive to many Mormons, including writer Lavina Fielding Anderson. She said, "News photos of counselors helping him [Benson] to wave or hold a shovel are deeply distressing." Along with others, she would like to see aging prophets be allowed to retire "so the LDS Church can continue its business."[19]

Criticism of LDS Church policy and doctrine led to the excommunication of Quinn and Anderson in September of 1993. In what was believed by many to be a "purge" encouraged by Mormon Apostle Boyd Packer, four other outspoken dissidents were also disciplined at that time.

This action was one of several reasons that compelled President Benson's grandson, Steve Benson, to resign from the LDS Church in late 1993. He accused LDS Church leaders of "destroying the spirituality of the very souls of its members" and of purposely misleading the Mormon people concerning the prophet's health.[20]

Benson, a Pulitzer Prize-winning editorial cartoonist for the *Arizona Republic* newspaper, decided to speak out when his then thirteen-year-old son asked him, "Dad, why do they call him prophet when he can't do anything?" It had, he said, been some time since his grandfather could participate in church affairs, "although that is an image that people deeply, almost desperately wanted to believe."[21] In July of 1993, he said:

> I believe the church strives mightily to perpetuate the myth, the fable, the fantasy that President Benson, if not operating on all cylinders, at least is functioning effectively enough . . . to be regarded by the Saints as a living, functioning prophet.[22]

In order to "perpetuate the myth," the *Salt Lake Tribune* reported:

> Photo sessions are managed closely to make the president appear younger and more vigorous. The church bureaucracy—including the president's counselors—recycle earlier speeches,

---

[18]Ibid.
[19]Ibid.
[20]*Salt Lake Tribune*, "Grandson of Prophet Asks to Be Removed From LDS Church Rolls," October 12, 1993, D-1.
[21]*Salt Lake Tribune*, July 10, 1993, p. E-3.
[22]*Salt Lake Tribune*, October 12, 1993, D-1.

Christmas messages, and even photos to complete the portrait.[23]

To question the prophet of Mormonism is akin to questioning God. Therefore, all LDS members are expected to give total allegiance to the leader in Salt Lake City. While Mormon prophets are looked upon as being above reproach, the Bible states that not even Peter himself was beyond criticism. As a result of Peter's inconsistent behavior among the Jews, Paul felt compelled to confront him face-to-face on the issue.[24]

As stated before, placing one's eternal trust in mortal men, such as the Mormon prophets and apostles, instead of the Bible is dangerous. Whereas man has been known to fail or to be wrong, it is only through God's Word that we can be assured that all doctrine and teachings are true.[25]

[23]*Salt Lake Tribune*, January 16, 1993, C–2.
[24]Galatians 2:11–12.
[25]For more information on Mormon prophets and apostles, please see Chapter 8 in *Answering Mormons' Questions*, Bethany House Publishers, 1991.

Why Does the Mormon Church Ignore Jesus' Role as Prophet of God's Church?

Mormon Apostle James Talmage once wrote:

> . . . the [LDS] Church holds itself in readiness to receive addi-
> tional light and knowledge "pertaining to the Kingdom of God"
> through divine revelation. . . . We rely therefore on the teachings
> of the living oracles of God as of equal validity with the doctrines
> of the written word.[1]

Modern-day revelation is of utmost importance to the Mormons
because their faith is based on the premise that their church is guided
by the current LDS prophet. One of the most often-cited criticisms
made by Mormons against Bible-believing Christians is that Christian
churches are not guided by a living prophet today. But is that true?

One of the more profound messianic prophecies in the Old Testament is found in Deuteronomy 18. In this chapter, Moses warns the
people to be on their guard against false prophets who proclaim themselves to be prophets of God. He predicted the coming of a prophet
who would resemble himself when he said:

---

[1]Talmage, *The Articles of Faith*, p. 7.

The Lord thy God will raise up unto thee a Prophet from the midst of thee, of thy brethren, like unto me; unto him ye shall hearken. . . . I will raise them up a Prophet from among their brethren, like unto thee, and will put my words in his mouth; and he shall speak unto them all that I shall command him. And it shall come to pass, that whosoever will not hearken unto my words which he shall speak in my name, I will require it of him.[2]

The Jews' willful ignorance of these passages caused the Lord to rebuke them, saying, "For had ye believed Moses, ye would have believed me: for he wrote of me."[3]

Following the miracle of the multiplied loaves and fishes, the people realized that Jesus was in fact "that prophet which should come into the world."[4] It was Moses' prophecy mentioned in Deuteronomy 18 that caused them to draw this conclusion.

The seventh chapter of John's gospel states that, on the last day of the Feast of Tabernacles, Jesus cried aloud:

If any man thirst, let him come unto Me, and drink. He that believeth on Me, as the scripture hath said, out of his belly shall flow rivers of living water.[5]

This comment apparently rang true to the people, for John 7:40 adds that "many of the people therefore, when they heard this saying, said, Of a truth this is the Prophet." Again, the prophet they spoke of—Jesus—was the one foretold by Moses in Deuteronomy 18.

Peter and John were used by the Lord to heal a man at the gate Beautiful. Such a miracle gained the attention of those present and, taking advantage of the situation, Peter presented a powerful sermon concerning the "Prince of life, whom God hath raised from dead."[6] Toward the end of his message, Peter reminded his audience:

Moses truly said unto the fathers, A prophet shall the Lord your God raise up unto you of your brethren, like unto me; him shall ye hear in all things whatsoever he shall say unto you. And it shall come to pass, that every soul, which will not hear that prophet,

---

[2]Deuteronomy 18:15–19.
[3]John 5:46.
[4]John 6:14.
[5]John 7:37–38.
[6]Acts 3:15.

shall be destroyed from among the people.[7]

Peter's message was clear. We must listen to the words of the prophet as prophesied by Moses. The martyr Stephen also gave reference to the Deuteronomy passage when he gave his defense to the Jews in Acts 7:37.

The bodily resurrection of Christ proves that He forever lives. Jesus is the final authority. To disregard His words is to bring destruction upon oneself. This fact, coupled with the aforementioned passages, demonstrates that Christ's church does have a living prophet guiding it today; His name is Jesus! He is to be our source of truth.

> God, who at sundry times and in divers manners, spake in time past unto the fathers by the prophets, Hath in these last days spoken unto us by His Son. . . .[8]

Our Lord said, "My sheep hear my voice."[9] Christ's true sheep do not listen to the voice of false prophets. True followers of Christ readily accept the revealed Word of God which has been a time-tested truth throughout the centuries and which Jesus said "would not pass away."[10]

> Therefore we ought to give the more earnest heed to the things which we have heard, lest at any time we should let them slip. . . . How shall we escape, if we neglect so great salvation; which at the first began to be spoken by the Lord, and was confirmed unto us by them that heard him.[11]

It is by God's Word, the Bible, that all things are compared, including the words of those who claim to be modern prophets.

---

[7]Acts 3:22–23.
[8]Hebrews 1:1–2.
[9]John 10:27.
[10]Matthew 24:35.
[11]Hebrews 2:1, 3.

NINE

Is the Mormon Priesthood Really of Ancient Origin?

The authority of the priesthood is so important to the Mormon that without it, its members do not have the "power and the authority of God given to men on earth to act in all things for the salvation of men."[1] The Mormon may even criticize the Christian and ask where his or her "authority" comes from. Mormon Apostle James Talmage wrote:

> No one may officiate in any ordinances of The Church of Jesus Christ of Latter-day Saints unless he has been ordained to the particular order or office of Priesthood, by those possessing the requisite authority. Thus, no man receives the Priesthood except under the hands of one who holds that Priesthood himself; that one must have obtained it from others previously commissioned; and so every bearer of the Priesthood today can trace his authority to the hands of Joseph Smith the Prophet, who received his ordination under the hands of the apostles Peter, James, and John; and they had been ordained by the Lord Jesus Christ.[2]

---

[1]*Gospel Principles*, p. 357.
[2]Talmage, *The Articles of Faith*, p. 189.

Mormonism teaches that all authority of the priesthood was "taken from the earth as the apostles of old were slain."[3] According to Mormon Apostle John Widtsoe, John the Baptist was probably the last to hold the Aaronic Priesthood, while the Melchizedek Priesthood ceased three or four centuries after Christ. Without these priesthoods, "there can be no true Church of Christ in its fullness."[4]

Thus, according to Mormonism, there was a 1700-year period when there was no authority and Christianity was in a state of total apostasy. Then, on May 15, 1829, it is claimed that the angelic John the Baptist appeared to the Mormon founder Joseph Smith and his scribe Oliver Cowdery. Using the authority given him by Peter, James, and John, the angel conferred upon them the "Priesthood of Aaron."[5]

In the 1833 *Book of Commandments*,[6] no mention is made of John the Baptist baptizing Joseph and Oliver. This section was initially published in the *Times and Seasons* on August 1, 1842, but it was not added to the *Doctrine and Covenants* (Section 13), until 1876.

There is also no mention of the Aaronic Priesthood in the *Book of Mormon*. Early Mormon Apostle Parley P. Pratt admitted that the Nephites did not have the Aaronic Priesthood when he said: ". . . the Aaronic Priesthood is no where pretended to in the *Book of Mormon*."[7] The *Book of Mormon* states the family of Lehi came from the tribe of Joseph.[8] Since the *Book of Mormon* also fails to mention the Melchizedek Priesthood, it appears that the Nephites were also acting without proper authority and did not represent "the true church."

As the story goes, Joseph and Oliver were later visited by Peter, James, and John. The three apostles bestowed upon Smith and Cowdery the next level of priesthood, known in Mormonism as the Melchizedek Priesthood.[9]

Without these two priesthoods, Mormonism teaches that men will have no chance at true salvation. As for each woman, her eternal progression is contingent on a priesthood-holding male. The problem with the idea that men have the opportunity to achieve the Aaronic

---

[3]Ibid., p. 188.
[4]Widtsoe, *Priesthood and Church Government*, pp. 19, 25, 45.
[5]D & C 13.
[6]The *Book of Commandments* became the *Doctrine and Covenants* in 1835.
[7]*Writings of Parley Parker Pratt*, p. 209.
[8]1 Nephi 5:16.
[9]D & C 27:12–13.

and Melchizedek Priesthoods is that it is without biblical precedence.

First, the idea that there was a total apostasy of Christendom for even one year (let alone 1700 years) is quite an outlandish statement. There have been devout Christians since the time of the apostles through all the ages. The Church of God has never disappeared. This fact verifies the truth of Jesus' statement when he said, "The gates of hell shall not prevail against" the Christian church.[10] If Christianity did disappear, it would not be possible for God to receive glory in the church "throughout all ages."[11]

While admitting that some past leaders of Christianity may have had pure motives and zeal, Mormon Apostle George Q. Cannon believed that a lack of priesthood meant they lacked the necessary authority. He stated:

> A Wesley, a Luther, a Calvin, a Wycliffe and a host of others who have arisen in the world, imbued with the highest and purest motives and the highest and most intense desires for the salvation of their fellow men, have labored zealously to turn men to God and to bring them to a knowledge of the Savior; but they have not had the authority of the Holy Priesthood.[12]

This is quite a presumptuous statement to make, but one that goes unnoticed by too many Christians who may feel Mormonism is no different from biblical Christianity. Consider that Mormonism teaches that this lack of authority applies to all non-Mormons today! John Widtsoe writes:

> The preaching of the Gospel also requires the authority of the Priesthood. Any person may teach righteous doctrine and will be blessed thereby. But only those who share in the power of the Priesthood can teach with authority the doctrines of Christ and invite the children of men into the Church of Christ. It is those

---

[10]Matthew 16:18. Mormon Apostle Orson Pratt said in 1850 that this verse refers only to the LDS Church. He said, "The gates of hell have prevailed and will continue to prevail over the Catholic mother of harlots, and over all her Protestant daughters; but as for the apostolic Church of Christ [Mormon Church], she rests secure in the mansion of eternal happiness, where she will remain until the apostate Catholic Church, with all her popes and bishops, together with all her harlot daughters shall be hurled down to hell" (*Divine Authenticity of the Book of Mormon*, No. 3, p. 44).

[11]Ephesians 3:21.

[12]Cannon, *Gospel Truth*, pp. 174–175.

who hold divine authority, that speak as they are "moved upon by the Holy Ghost" (D & C 68:3).[13]

Speaking of the LDS Church, he explained:

> The Church itself is a product of Priesthood. Therefore, whenever the Church of Christ is upon earth the Priesthood is a part of it. The Church is the instrument through which Priesthood operates. Men may then obtain the Priesthood through the Church and in no other way.[14]

James Talmage, another Mormon apostle, added:

> The special privileges and blessings associated with the Church, the right to hold and exercise the Priesthood with its boundless possibilities and eternal powers, will be, as now they are, for those only who enter into the covenant and become part of the Church of Jesus Christ.[15]

Second, the Old Testament teaches that the Aaronic Priesthood could be held only by certain men who came from the Levite tribe, which had its roots in Aaron, the brother of Moses.[16] It was a hereditary priesthood, one which would invalidate the non-Jewish Smith and Cowdery as well as all subsequent non-Jewish Mormons.

Despite not coming from the tribe of Levi, the New Testament says Jesus fulfilled this priesthood. Hebrews 7:11–14 says:

> If therefore perfection were by the Levitical priesthood, (under it the people received the law,) what further need was there that another priest should rise after the order of Melchisedec, and not be called after the order of Aaron? *For the priesthood being changed*, there is made of necessity a change also of the law. For he of whom these things are spoken pertaineth to another tribe, of which no man gave attendance at the altar. For it is evident that our Lord sprang out of Judah; of which tribe Moses spake nothing concerning priesthood.[17]

According to the author of Hebrews, the Aaronic Priesthood was

---

[13]Widtsoe, *Priesthood and Church Government*, p. 41.
[14]Ibid., p. 45.
[15]Talmage, *The Articles of Faith*, p. 368.
[16]See Numbers 3:10–11 as well as *D & C* 107:16.
[17]Emphasis ours.

inadequate to bring salvation to men and therefore was no longer necessary due to the Great Sacrifice of Christ. This is why New Testament Christians have never had to utilize the temple and sacrifice lambs and bulls. All of the sacrifices in the Old Testament were merely foreshadowing the blood, which was to be paid by Christ, the Lamb of God. Therefore, the Mormon idea that the Aaronic Priesthood is necessary becomes a moot point.

Christian scholar Alfred Edersheim noted that the duties of the Levites included keeping the sanctuary clean, guarding the temple, and making sure the gates were either opened or closed at their proper times. It was also the duty of the Levites to prevent those who were defiled from entering the sanctuary.[18]

Though a Levite did not have to necessarily be a priest, a priest had to be a Levite. The hereditary line had to be proven in order for a candidate to be approved. Dr. Edersheim noted that should a candidate for the office of priest fail to prove his legitimacy, "the candidate was dressed and veiled in black, and permanently removed."[19] He wrote:

> If he passed that ordeal, inquiry was next made as to any physical defects, of which Maimonides enumerates a hundred and forty that permanently, and twenty-two which temporarily disqualified [him] for the exercise of the priestly office.[20]

The function of the priest was to officiate in the sacrifices and to also offer counsel ranging from military advice to interpretation of Israelite custom and law. The priesthood in Mormonism is not an identical counterpart.

Today, twelve-year-old Mormon boys are baptized into the Aaronic Priesthood and given the title "Deacon." This is especially interesting since 1 Timothy 3:12 says that "deacons [are to] be husbands of one wife, ruling their children and their own houses well." Even Joseph Smith seemed to feel that grown men should be the ones who receive the Aaronic Priesthood since he said that ". . . the deacons and teachers should be appointed to watch over the church, to be standing ministers unto the church."[21] Second LDS President Brigham Young

---

[18]Alfred Edersheim, *The Temple*, p. 89.
[19]Ibid., p. 95.
[20]Ibid.
[21]*D & C* 84:111.

claimed that deacons were even to be married:

> It is not the business of an ignorant young man, of no experi-
> ence in family matters, to inquire into the circumstances of fami-
> lies, and know the wants of every person . . . it is not the business
> of boys to do this; but select a man who has got a family to be a
> Deacon, whose wife can go with him, and assist him in adminis-
> tering to the needy in the ward. . . . I will venture to say the view I
> take of the matter is not to be disputed or disproved by Scripture
> or reason.[22]

However, tenth LDS President Joseph Fielding Smith disagreed
with Young's interpretation of 1 Timothy 3:12 and said it should no
longer apply today. Several paragraphs after claiming that the New
Testament office of "pastor" is not necessary because it can be applied
to other LDS positions, Smith contradicted both Joseph Smith and
Young when he wrote:

> It was the judgment of Paul that a deacon in that day should be
> a married man. That does not apply to our day. Conditions were
> different in the days of Paul. In that day a minister was not consid-
> ered qualified to take part in the ministry until he was 30 years of
> age. Under those conditions deacons, teachers, and priests were
> mature men. This is not the requirement today.[23]

What conditions have changed that would make today's younger
people more qualified than those in ancient times? Better yet, what
conditions have changed since the time Brigham Young said a deacon
should be married?

Regarding a fixed age requirement for the Aaronic Priesthood, Dr.
Edersheim wrote:

> There was not any fixed age for entering on the office of high-
> priest, any more than on that of an ordinary priest. The Talmudists
> put it down at twenty years. But the unhappy descendant of the
> Maccabees, Aritobulus, was only sixteen years of age when his
> beauty, as he officiated as high-priest in the temple, roused the
> jealousy of Herod, and procured his death. The entrance of the
> Levites is fixed, in the sacred text, at thirty during the wilderness

---

[22]*Journal of Discourses* 2:89.
[23]Joseph Fielding Smith, *Doctrines of Salvation* 3:109–110.

period, and after that, when the work would require less bodily strength, but a larger number of ministers, at twenty-five years of age.[24]

Not only is the function of the LDS priesthood different from that of ancient times, the method of ordination is different as well. Leviticus chapter 8 gives elaborate details as to how the priest was to be consecrated for service. This complex rite included ceremonial washings, corporate prayer over the head of the sacrificial bullock, the slaying of the bullock, the sprinkling of its blood, and the burning of the sacrifice. This was followed by the sacrifice of two rams and the offering of bread. The initiates were then separated from the people for seven days in which they would perform numerous animal sacrifices. On the eighth day, they would again emerge to offer sacrifice and bless the people. If the Mormon Priesthood is a restoration of the ancient priesthood, why are their priests not set apart in a similar fashion?

Third, the office of the Melchizedek Priesthood is held by only one person. His name? Jesus Christ.

Hebrews 7:21–24 says:

> (For those priests were made without an oath; but this with an oath by him that said unto him, The Lord sware and will not repent, Thou art a priest for ever after the order of Melchisedec:) By so much was Jesus made a surety of a better testament. And they truly were many priests, because they were not suffered to continue by reason of death: But this man, because he continueth ever, hath an unchangeable priesthood.

Although a priest named Melchizedek is talked about in Genesis 14, there is little information on his background. Like Christ, there is no evidence of his priestly succession or of his priestly parentage. There is no evidence in the entire Bible of anyone but Jesus being called a priest after the order of Melchizedek. Mormon leaders may continue to assume that men like Peter, James, and John held this office, but such claims are completely without biblical support.

The old order of the Aaronic Priesthood was fulfilled in Jesus since He became our mediator to God the Father.[25] He is "holy, harmless,

---

[24]Edersheim, *The Temple*, pp. 94–95.
[25]1 Timothy 2:5.

undefiled, separate from sinners." Therefore, we do not need a human priest who needs to be cleansed first before he could offer sacrifice to cleanse others. This was done once by Christ when He offered up Himself on the cross.[26]

Instead of being handed a priesthood whose function has passed, Christians are given what is known as a "royal priesthood" under Jesus.[27] While the Aaronic Priesthood could be held by a very few people whose primary function was to sacrifice animals on behalf of the sins of the people, the Royal Priesthood is open to all believers. Its function is to offer spiritual sacrifices acceptable to God through Jesus Christ. This office gives believers the right or authority to become the sons of God.[28]

Fourth, when it comes to the office of High Priest, Mormonism again diverges from the historical norm by having a multitude of men simultaneously holding this position. The Bible does not support the idea that more than one person held the office of high priest at the same time. Dr. Edersheim wrote:

> Originally the office of high-priest was regarded as being held for life and hereditary; but the troubles of later times made it a matter of cabal, crime, or bribery.[29]

Alma 13:10, in the *Book of Mormon*, states that "there were many who were ordained and became high priests of God." One LDS Church manual states:

> High priests hold the keys of presiding over the affairs of the kingdom, and thus General Authorities, stake presidencies, bishoprics, and patriarchs are ordained as high priests. The quorum of high priests consist of all high priests in a stake with no maximum number.[30]

This is a clear contradiction of the biblical pattern. While a Mormon may retreat to Luke 3:2,[31] history shows that Annas held the high priesthood from around A.D. 6–15. Five of his sons also held

---

[26]Hebrews 7:26–27.
[27]See 1 Peter 2:9–10 and Hebrews 4:14.
[28]John 1:12.
[29]Edersheim, *The Temple*, p. 94.
[30]*Doctrine and Covenants Student Manual*, p. 436.
[31]It says that ". . . Annas and Caiaphas being the high priests. . . ."

this position, including his son-in-law Caiaphas who was appointed by the Roman government in A.D. 18. Caiaphas held this position until around A.D. 36. Luke 3:2 poses no problem because the former high priest retained his title even though he no longer acted in that capacity.

Jesus Christ offered himself "once for all" for the sins of the people.[32] The duty of the high priest to stand in the gap on behalf of the people has therefore been transferred to Jesus Christ "who ever liveth to make intercession" for us. He alone is our great high priest.

Only eighteen men held the office of high priest during the time of Solomon's temple. If a single man held this office for a lifetime, it would make sense that only a few would have held this position.

Solomon's temple was burned by the Babylonians and later rebuilt by Zerubbabel. It was around 20 B.C. that Herod the Great proceeded to rebuild and enlarge the Jerusalem temple. While the exact number is not known, it is estimated that as many as eighty-five men served in the capacity of high priest in Herod's temple until it was destroyed by the Romans in A.D. 70.

As explained by Dr. Edersheim, the large number of high priests was due to the corruption of the system at that time. Instead of being governed by Scripture and tradition, this office became one of power, money, and influence. When the temple was destroyed, there was no longer a need for the priesthood since its entire purpose revolved around the temple.

In summary, Christianity rests on the fact that Jesus fulfilled the incomplete Aaronic Priesthood. Each one of us, through faith in Christ, has the right to be called a child of God with full authority to approach the throne of grace.

---

[32]See Hebrews 10:10.

T E N

Where in the Bible Does It Say a Person Has to Be Worthy to Enter the Temple?

Tenth Mormon President Joseph Fielding Smith stated:

> Of course there are people who are not worthy to go to the temple, and therefore should not go to the temple. No one should go to the temple except those who are worthy. . . .[1]

A similar thought is found on page 48 in the full-color LDS Church publication entitled *Temples of the Church of Jesus Christ of Latter-day Saints*. It says that "no unclean person has the right to enter God's house." These quotes illustrate an important facet of the Mormon religion: while temple participation is important, it is not intended for those who do not live up to the standards of the LDS Church.

The road to worthiness involves adherence to a list of requirements ranging from regular attendance of meetings and paying a full tithe, to not drinking coffee or tea. A temple recommend is an identification card, entitling the bearer to enter a Mormon temple. It is issued only to Mormons who have met these and other conditions.

Since Jesus' death and resurrection, the Christian church has

---

[1]Joseph Fielding Smith, *Doctrines of Salvation* 2:61

taught that temple worship and animal sacrifices are no longer required. Jesus' blood is the atoning sacrifice that makes it possible to obtain salvation.[2] If the LDS Church leaders want to teach that temple worship was restored by latter-day revelation less than two centuries ago, then we should find more similarities than differences when comparing temple worship from Bible days and temple worship as practiced in Mormonism today.

The differences are numerous. For instance, the temple in Bible days was created for sacrifice, both animal and grain. Today, the LDS Church performs no such sacrifices. There was only one temple in Bible days, which was located in Jerusalem. Currently, the LDS Church has dozens of temples, which are found throughout the world. The Bible never mentions the idea that Christians or Jews performed baptisms for the dead,[3] marriages for eternity, or temple endowments in the Jerusalem temple. Yet these are the main functions of the Mormon temples.

Although the above demonstrates the contrast between the temple of Bible days and the Mormon temples, perhaps the biggest difference is the idea of who should be allowed entrance into these buildings. While the LDS Church demands its followers to be "worthy" in order to participate in its temples, the Bible gives a clear picture that a sense of unworthiness was much more preferred by God than a false feeling of virtue.

The Gospel of Luke tells the story of two men who went to the temple to pray; one was a Pharisee, the other a publican (or tax collector). The Pharisee prayed:

> God, I thank thee, that I am not as other men are, extortioners, unjust, adulterers, or even as this publican. I fast twice in the week, I give tithes of all that I possess.[4]

The Pharisee's attitude is not uncommon among many sincere people who erroneously think that their "good works" impress an all-holy God. The publican's demeanor was entirely different. Knowing that he was sinful and undeserving of God's notice, he approached

---

[2] Among many references to these points, consider Romans 3:25; 5:9; Ephesians 1:7; 2:13; Colossians 1:20; Hebrews 9; 1 Peter 1:19; 1 John 1:7.
[3] See the chapter on baptism for the dead in this book.
[4] Luke 18:11–12.

God in the temple by praying, "God be merciful to me a sinner."[5] His attitude, not the attitude of the Pharisee, caused our Lord to comment, "This man went down to his house justified rather than the other."[6]

Tax collectors in ancient Israel were known to have unscrupulous business practices and were despised by the Jewish population. According to Dr. Donald A. Hagner of Fuller Theological Seminary:

> In this system one usually became a tax collector by bidding against others to guarantee the highest amount of money to the tax-farmers (the true *publicani*), who were directly responsible to the Roman government. This arrangement obviously provided the opportunity at several levels for considerable personal gain through the unrestricted inflation of taxes and tolls, a portion of which conveniently went into the pockets of the middlemen.[7]

Dr. Hagner points out that tax collectors were rendered ceremoniously unclean because of their regular contact with Gentiles and were commonly linked with "sinners."[8] Certainly, if temple "recommends" were required in biblical times, this publican would not have qualified under today's Mormon guidelines. If worthiness has always been a requirement to enter a temple, how did the publican of Luke 18 get in?

Evidence that temple Mormonism has nothing in common with the temple worship in Jerusalem comes from the fact that the temple's entire purpose was to meet the needs of unworthy sinners. The penitent Jew would come to the temple to offer sacrifice for his sins and the sins of his family. The sacrifice would be given to the priest who would stand in the gap between the sinner and God.

On the Day of Atonement, the High Priest would first offer a sacrifice for himself. Christian scholar Alfred Edersheim states that the High Priest would lay his hands on the sacrificial bull and pray as follows:

> Ah, JEHOVAH! I have committed iniquity; I have transgressed; I have sinned—I and my house. Oh, then, JEHOVAH, I entreat

---

[5]Luke 18:13.
[6]Luke 18:14.
[7]*International Standard Bible Encyclopedia* 4:742.
[8]See Matthew 11:19; Mark 2:15; Luke 15:1.

Thee, cover over the iniquities, the transgressions, and the sins which I have committed, transgressed, and sinned before Thee.[9]

Does the prayer of the High Priest on the Day of Atonement sound like the prayer of a man who feels he is worthy?

Later, a similar prayer would be repeated by the High Priest on behalf of the people.

The concept of temple worthiness has been blamed for causing many hard feelings between non-Mormon parents and their Mormon children. Faithful Latter-day Saints are encouraged to be married in Mormon temples; however, because worthiness is a requirement for entrance, non-Mormon parents are not allowed to be a part of one of the most blessed events in the lives of their children.

Although few Mormons would freely admit it, temple Mormonism fosters a class society and feeds the ego of those who hold temple recommends. The fact that these Mormons are found "worthy" places them in a class above those who do not hold recommends. Like the Pharisee of Luke 18, this sinful attitude of pride can easily become a reality in the Mormon's life.

The true Gospel message leaves no room for pride because our salvation was purchased through the righteousness of Christ. When Paul said our salvation was "not of works, lest any man should boast,"[10] he confirmed the fact that God himself is the author and finisher of our faith. Even the faith to believe comes as a gift from God.

Many Mormons fail to realize that the temple and its priesthood was a foreshadowing of the coming Great High Priest, Jesus Christ. Upon His death, the temple veil was ripped in two.[11] This symbolizes the fact that believers can now directly approach the throne of God. Apart from the righteousness of Christ, all our "righteous acts" are like filthy rags.[12] Faith in His unspotted righteousness, not our personal merit, makes all believers worthy in the sight of God.

---

[9]Edersheim, *The Temple*, p. 310.
[10]Ephesians 2:8.
[11]Luke 23:45.
[12]Isaiah 64:6.

ELEVEN

What Historical Support Does the Mormon Church Have to Justify Baptism for the Dead?

A great majority of the work that is performed in LDS temples throughout the world by faithful Mormons is done on behalf of the dead. Besides endowments for the dead, baptisms for the dead are also performed.

The Mormon Church boasts that its members have performed ordinances on behalf of such notables as William Shakespeare, George Washington, Abraham Lincoln, Patrick Henry, Paul Revere, Leo Tolstoy, and Dwight Eisenhower, to name a few.[1] While hundreds of millions of dollars have been spent on LDS temples, millions of hours have been spent on genealogical research as Mormons trace their family lines so baptisms for deceased relatives may be performed.

Genealogical records are maintained in the LDS Church's massive Family History Library, west of Salt Lake City's Temple Square. It's continually replenished with data from 150 countries, via birth, marriage, and death certificates; records from other countries such as christenings and baptisms; old train and ship passenger lists;

---

[1]*Salt Lake Tribune*, "Baptism for Dead Adds Lincoln, Tolstoy to LDS Ranks," August 17, 1992, A-6. This article stated "several thousand baptisms for the dead are conducted daily" in LDS temples worldwide.

census, military, immigration, and court records, including wills, probates and deeds; and Social Security death records . . . information comes from so many sources, and the computer system is so sophisticated, there is no way a person can be excluded by request.[2]

Vicarious baptism is the key ordinance performed on behalf of the dead. Its importance to Mormonism was stressed by tenth Mormon President Joseph Fielding Smith when he wrote:

> If we wilfully neglect the salvation of our dead, then also we shall stand rejected of the Lord, because we have rejected our dead; and just so sure their blood will be required at our hands. . . . But the greatest and grandest duty of all is to labor for the dead . . . we cannot be saved without them.[3]

Mormonism allows the faithful Mormon to be baptized by proxy on behalf of deceased relatives who did not embrace Mormon teaching during their lifetime. It is through this act, Mormons are told, that their ancestors will be given the opportunity to respond to the Mormon message in the spirit world.

While Mormonism teaches that Jesus' death paved the way for salvation, it is taught that the person who is baptized by proxy for another becomes the "savior" of that person. At the Spring 1993 General Conference, Mormon Apostle David B. Haight spoke on the doctrine of baptism for the dead:

> All of these activities help provide the sacred ordinances of the temple for your ancestors. If you will do this, you will know the indescribable joy of being a savior on Mount Zion to a waiting ancestor whom you have helped.[4]

However, just being baptized for a dead person does not guarantee that he or she will accept the Mormon gospel in this state. Heber C. Kimball, a member of the First Presidency in Brigham Young's day, said:

> Perhaps my father may not receive the Gospel. If he don't (sic), my baptism will not do him any good. . . . You might as well go

[2]Ibid.
[3]Joseph Fielding Smith, *Doctrines of Salvation* 2:145, 149.
[4]*Ensign*, May 1993, p. 25.

and be baptized for a devil as for a man who will not receive the Gospel in the spirit world.[5]

Baptism for the dead did not become an issue in Mormonism until 1840. It was in this year Joseph Smith stated:

> I first mentioned the doctrine in public when preaching the funeral sermon of Brother Seymour Brunson; and have since then given general instruction in the Church on the subject.[6]

Smith would later proclaim:

> This doctrine was the burden of the scriptures. Those Saints who neglect it in behalf of their deceased relatives, do it at the peril of their own salvation. . . . The greatest responsibility in this world that God has laid upon us is to seek after our dead.[7]

This teaching allowed his followers to have a peace of mind about their ancestors who lived between the ages of the "Great Apostasy" (soon after Jesus' apostles died) and the early nineteenth century when Mormonism was founded. However, he never intended this to allow everyone *after* 1830, who had already heard the Mormon gospel, to have a second chance at the celestial kingdom. Today, many Mormons are baptized for their recently deceased relatives who had every chance to accept the Mormon gospel. Said Smith:

> The Saints have the privilege of being baptized for those of their relatives who are dead, whom they believe would have embraced the Gospel, if they had been privileged with hearing it, and who have received the Gospel in the spirit, through the instrumentality of those who have been commissioned to preach to them while in prison.[8]

Mormonism teaches that baptism for the dead is for the benefit of those who did not (or do not today) have the opportunity to hear and accept the Mormon gospel or where there are no "legal administrators."

As mentioned, many Mormons are baptized every day on behalf of

---

[5]*Journal of Discourses* 5:90.
[6]*Documentary History of the Church* 4:231.
[7]Joseph Fielding Smith, editor, *Teachings of the Prophet Joseph Smith*, pp. 193, 356.
[8]Ibid., p. 179.

their relatives who have lived during the past century in America and other lands where Mormonism is easily found. Even though their grandparents or other relatives rejected Mormonism, these Mormons apparently believe that these relatives could still have a second chance to attain the celestial kingdom through baptism for the dead. This is not a consistent view nor is it one that the LDS Church seems to support. Joseph Fielding Smith admitted:

> Salvation for the dead is grossly misunderstood by many of the Latter-day Saints . . . the Lord did *not* offer to those who had *every* opportunity while in this mortal existence the privilege of *another* chance in the world of spirits.[9]

In a funeral service in 1878, Joseph F. Smith—who later became the sixth Mormon president—said:

> We have a certain work to do in order to liberate those who, because of their ignorance and the unfavorable circumstances in which they were placed while here, are unprepared for eternal life; we have to open the door for them, by performing ordinances which they cannot perform for themselves, and which are essential to their release from the "prison-house". . . .[10]

Joseph Fielding Smith wrote:

> If the person had every opportunity to receive these blessings in person and refused, or through procrastination and lack of faith did not receive them, then he is not entitled to them, and it is doubtful if the work for him will be valid if done within one week [after death] or 1,000 years.[11]

He added that baptism for the dead was

> For those who died without having had the opportunity to hear and receive the gospel; also, for those who were faithful members of the Church who lived in foreign lands or where, during their lifetime, they did not have the privilege to go to a temple, yet they were converted and were true members of the Church. The work for the dead is not intended for those who had every opportunity

---

[9]Joseph Fielding Smith, *Doctrines of Salvation* 2:184, (emphasis his).
[10]*Journal of Discourses* 19:264.
[11]Joseph Fielding Smith, *Doctrines of Salvation* 2:179.

to receive it, who had it taught to them, and who then refused to receive it, or had not interest enough to attend to these ordinances when they were living.[12]

This is why Bruce McConkie denounced the idea that baptism for the dead was a second chance to gain salvation:

There is no such thing as a second chance to gain salvation by accepting the gospel in the spirit world after spurning, declining, or refusing to accept it in this life. It is true that there may be a second chance to hear and accept the gospel, but those who have thus procrastinated their acceptance of the saving truths will not gain salvation in the celestial kingdom of God.[13]

Spencer Kimball, the twelfth LDS president, said those who have heard the Mormon message have had their chance:

It must be remembered that vicarious work for the dead is for those who could not do the work for themselves. Men and women who live in mortality and who have heard the gospel here have had their day. . . .[14]

Many Mormons live with the misconception that they can perform proxy baptisms on behalf of their deceased relatives who rejected Mormonism in order to ensure being together as a family in eternity. This is not supported by LDS teaching. The family unit is preserved only in the top level of the celestial kingdom and only if every family member has kept all the commandments. McConkie states that those who reject the Mormon gospel in this life and reverse their course and accept it in the spirit world will go no further than the second level of Mormon heaven known as the terrestrial kingdom.[15]

The LDS Church claims baptism for the dead has its roots in the Old Testament. If baptism for the dead is the "most glorious subject" pertaining to the everlasting gospel, one should expect that its practice would at least be given a slight mention either in the Bible itself

[12]Smith, *Doctrines of Salvation* 2:184, (emphasis his).
[13]McConkie, *Mormon Doctrine*, p. 685.
[14]Spencer W. Kimball, *The Miracle of Forgiveness*, p. 314.
[15]McConkie, *Mormon Doctrine*, p. 784.

or in rabbinical writings such as the Mishnah or Talmud.[16]

Mormons are told that vicarious baptisms for the dead can only be performed in one of the many temples owned by the LDS Church. However, Joseph Fielding Smith admitted that there was no historical precedence for this. He believed baptisms for the dead were never performed in the Jerusalem temple but were performed "elsewhere."[17]

Every temple owned by the Church of Jesus Christ of Latter-day Saints contains a baptismal font that resembles the brazen sea mentioned in 1 Kings 7:23. The brazen sea replaced the bronze laver of the tabernacle and consisted of a large font resting on the backs of twelve oxen. The diameter of the font measured over fourteen feet across, weighed approximately 30 tons, and could hold around 12,000 gallons of water.

Supporting the font were twelve figures resembling oxen. The number twelve represents the twelve tribes of Israel. The oxen were placed in four groups of three, each group facing a different point of the compass (three faced the north, three faced the south, etc.). While many Latter-day Saints feel that baptizing by proxy in a similar font is a restored practice from early Christianity, Joseph Fielding Smith downplayed this notion. He wrote:

> This font, or brazen sea, was not used for baptisms for the dead, for there were no baptisms for the dead until after the resurrection of the Lord. It is a logical venture to say that it was used for baptizing the living for the remission of their sins.[18]

History challenges Smith's assumption regarding this font being used for baptisms for the living. Solomon's brazen sea would only remain intact for about 250 years when it was altered by King Ahaz; he removed the oxen and placed the sea on a "pavement of stones."[19] During the reign of King Zedekiah (circa 600 B.C.), the sea was broken into pieces and carried off to Babylon.[20] While the Jews did continue the use of a laver, they never attempted to recreate one to resemble Solomon's brazen sea. Therefore, there was no brazen sea during

---

[16]The Mishnah is a compilation of Jewish oral law that is divided into six categories. The Talmud serves as a commentary on the Mishnah.
[17]Joseph Fielding Smith, *Doctrines of Salvation* 2:169.
[18]Joseph Fielding Smith, *Answers to Gospel Questions* 5:13.
[19]2 Kings 16:17.
[20]2 Kings 25:13.

the time following Jesus' resurrection.

There is no historical support for the idea that the brazen sea or the laver were ever used for baptisms of any sort. Second Chronicles 4:6 says that the sea was exclusively used for the priests' ceremonial washings.

As far as LDS Scripture is concerned, there are few references to which a Mormon may turn in order to support this doctrine of vicarious baptism. The primary proof text is 1 Corinthians 15:29.[21] This passage reads:

> Else what shall they do which are baptized for the dead, if the dead rise not at all? why are they then baptized for the dead.

Unlike the surrounding context, Paul uses the third person form here in order to exclude himself and true believers. Notice: "Else what shall *they* do. . . ." It would seem reasonable that, if baptism for the dead is truly the most glorious subject pertaining to the everlasting gospel, and if Paul actually performed the ritual himself, he would not have purposely switched to the third person plural and used the word "they," thereby excluding himself.[22]

While not mentioning baptism for the dead, another verse used by some Mormons is Hebrews 11:40. It reads, "God having provided some better thing for us, that they without us should not be made perfect." Joseph Smith explained this text by saying:

> . . . these are principles in relation to the dead and the living . . . their salvation is necessary and essential to our salvation, as Paul says concerning the fathers—that they without us cannot be made perfect—neither can we without our dead be made perfect . . . what is that subject? It is the baptism for the dead. For we without them cannot be made perfect; neither can they without us be made perfect.[23]

In drawing this conclusion, Smith ignores his 1833 re-translation of this verse. His *Inspired Version* of the Bible reads:

> God having provided some better things for them through their

---

[21]Other LDS proof texts are *D & C* 124, 127–128.
[22]For a complete description of this issue, please refer to Chapter 28 in *Answering Mormons' Questions*, Bethany House Publishers, 1991.
[23]*D & C* 128:15,18.

sufferings, for without *sufferings* they could not be made perfect.[24]

According to Smith's *Inspired Version*, it was an individual's sufferings that brought about perfection, not a vicarious baptism.

Amazingly enough, not even the *Book of Mormon*—claimed by Joseph Smith to contain the "fulness of the everlasting Gospel"—gives historical evidence to this practice. While the words "baptism," "baptize," "baptized," and "baptizing" appear numerous times, "baptism for the dead" or an equivalent is never mentioned. In fact, there are passages within the *Book of Mormon* that seem to contradict this concept.[25]

With so much expense incurred and effort given to baptism for the dead by the LDS Church, it seems peculiar that there is a major lack of biblical backing to support this keystone Mormon doctrine.[26] Milton R. Hunter, a former member of the First Council of the Seventy, explained one possible reason when he said:

> This doctrine was so well known by Jesus' apostles and the members of the Christian Church during the Apostolic Age that Paul need not explain the doctrine in detail when he wrote to the Saints.[27]

Again the Mormon scholar must turn to the argument of silence. If Paul did not need to explain "well known" doctrines in detail, it is a wonder such important doctrines as faith, grace, and the atonement of Christ were ever mentioned at all. To the contrary, if baptism for the dead is such a vital doctrine as the LDS Church would have its members believe, then one would expect to find many additional biblical references to support it.

Regarding early church history, there is no outside proof to show that baptism for the dead was accepted by the early Christian Church. According to New Testament scholar G. W. Bromiley, apart from a possible yet obscure reference made by Tertullian, a second-century theologian, there is evidence of such a practice only among heretical

---

[24]Hebrews 11:40, *Inspired Version*, (emphasis ours).
[25]See 2 Nephi 9:38; Mosiah 3:25, 16:5,11; 26:25–27; Alma 34:32–35.
[26]See 2 Corinthians 6:2; 1 Timothy 1:3–4; Titus 3:9; Hebrews 9:27.
[27]Hunter, *The Gospel Through the Ages*, p. 224.

groups like the Cerinthians and the Marcionites.[28]

It is unfortunate that the doctrine of baptism for the dead is accepted at face value by many Mormons who have not researched the roots of this essential LDS teaching.

---

[28]*International Standard Bible Encyclopedia* 1:426. Cerinthus was a gnostic antagonist of the apostle John who denied the Virgin Birth and taught of a coming millennium of unrestrained sensuality. Marcion was excommunicated as a heretic in A.D. 144. He had his own edited version of the Scriptures, which excluded the Old Testament and much of the New Testament. He refused baptism to married persons and, like the Mormons, used water instead of wine for the Lord's Supper (2:489–90).

TWELVE

If Mormon Families Will Be Together Forever, Where Will the In-Laws Live?

A common expression within the Latter-day Saint Church is that "Families are Forever." This promise of eternal togetherness is given to all Mormons who faithfully live up to the conditions of the LDS Church.

Former Mormon Apostle George Q. Cannon wrote at the turn of the century:

> If I have children, if I have a wife, I shall have them in eternity. I shall preside over that family no matter how small it may be or how large it may extend. They will be my kingdom; for this is the promise of God.[1]

Faithful Latter-day Saints view their present condition as "gods in embryo." As a result of their individual righteousness, they hope one day to blossom into full-fledged godhood. Lest it be argued that this idea no longer exists in Mormonism, consider the following quote by Mormon writer Terry J. Moyer:

---

[1]Cannon, *Gospel Truth*, p. 93. Cannon also said that further procreation, or "the greatest power that man possesses on the earth," will take place in this future state.

The stunning truth, lost to humankind before the Restoration, is that each of us is a god in embryo. We may become as our heavenly parents. We, too, in exalted families, may one day preside in our own realms, under him who is our God and our Father forever.[2]

In order to reach this exalted state, there are a number of requirements that a person must meet in order to achieve an eternal kingdom where the family unit will dwell. One of the most important conditions is celestial (meaning temple) marriage. According to sections 131 and 132 of the LDS scripture *Doctrine and Covenants*:

In the celestial glory there are three heavens or degrees; And in order to obtain the highest, a man must enter into this order of the priesthood [meaning the new and everlasting covenant of marriage]; And if he does not, he cannot obtain it. He may enter into the other, but that is the end of his kingdom; he cannot have an increase.[3]

And again, verily I say unto you, if a man marry a wife by my word, which is my law, and by the new and everlasting covenant, and it is sealed unto them by the Holy Spirit of promise. . . . Ye shall come forth in the first resurrection; and if it be after the first resurrection, in the next resurrection; and shall inherit thrones, kingdoms, principalities, powers and dominions. . . .[4]

In this context, "increase" is the ability to procreate. Mormon leadership teaches that the celestial kingdom will provide an opportunity for the family to procreate and rule its own planet in the same way God and His heavenly wives have dominion over the planet Earth. It is only through marriage—temple marriage, to be exact[5]—that this goal of the celestial kingdom can be accomplished. Twelfth Mormon President Spencer W. Kimball stated:

If one is going to be in God's kingdom of exaltation, where God dwells in all his glory, one will be there as a husband or a wife and not otherwise. Regardless of his virtues, the single person, or the

---

[2]*Ensign*, June 1993, p. 10.
[3]*D & C* 131:1–4.
[4]Ibid., 132:19.
[5]*Gospel Principles*, p. 222. Only those marriages that take place in the temple will continue forever. All other marriages end at death.

one married for this life only, cannot be exalted. All normal people should marry and rear families.[6]

While striving to be together for eternity as a family may sound like a reasonable goal, the Mormon concept has many flaws. One point that many Saints may never think about regarding this doctrine is that the Mormon family can be together only if each one of them is exalted to the same level of LDS heaven. The following areas are true according to Mormonism:

1. There are three levels of heaven (celestial, terrestrial, and telestial);

2. Within the top level, or celestial kingdom, there are three levels;[7]

3. A person can reach godhood only by making it to the very top level within the celestial kingdom. This level is called the "Church of the Firstborn."

If these points are true, it would therefore be necessary to have all members of a family unit be worthy enough to reach this top level of the celestial kingdom if they want to be together forever.

Before going any further, let's examine the idea of the "Church of the Firstborn." Former LDS Apostle James Talmage gave a description of those Mormons who would enter this level:

> There are some who have striven to obey all the divine commandments, who have accepted the testimony of Christ, obeyed "the laws and ordinances of the Gospel," and received the Holy Spirit; these are they who have overcome evil by godly works and who are therefore entitled to the highest glory; these belong to the Church of the Firstborn, unto whom the Father has given all things. . . .[8]

Tenth Mormon President Joseph Fielding Smith commented on this subject by saying:

> Exalted beings belong to Church of the Firstborn. Those who gain exaltation in the celestial kingdom are those who are members of the Church of the Firstborn; in other words, those who keep *all* the commandments of the Lord. There will be many who are mem-

[6]Spencer W. Kimball, *The Miracle of Forgiveness*, p. 245.
[7]For the first two points, see *Mormon Doctrine*, pp. 116–117, 778, 784.
[8]Talmage, *The Articles of Faith*, pp. 91–92.

bers of the Church of Jesus Christ of Latter-day Saints who shall *never* become members of the Church of the Firstborn.[9]

Smith also said that the family unit is able to continue only in the celestial kingdom. He wrote:

> Outside of the celestial kingdom there is no family organization. That organization is reserved for those who are willing to abide in *every covenant* and *every obligation* which we are called upon to receive while we sojourn here in this mortal life.[10]

Notice in the above quotes that *complete* obedience to the law is required for such a position. If a family member failed to be morally pure during his or her earthly existence, this level would not be procured.

Some Mormons have erroneously assumed that, through the process of eternal progression, every Mormon will someday be joined together as a family. However, twelfth President Spencer W. Kimball stated this is not likely since "jumping levels" is an impossibility. He wrote:

> After a person has been assigned to his place in the kingdom, either in the telestial, the terrestrial or the celestial, or to his exaltation, he will never advance from his assigned glory to another glory. That is eternal! That is why we must make our decisions early in life and why it is imperative that such decisions be right.[11]

The family member who does not prepare for exaltation in this life will be doomed to spend eternity in another level of Mormon heaven. In other words, each family member must strictly obey every one of God's commandments. Joseph Fielding Smith added:

> The exaltation to the celestial kingdom is so great that the Father is fully justified in making it dependent upon strict obedience to *all* of his commandments. The celestial kingdom is a kingdom of perfection.[12]

---

[9]Joseph Fielding Smith, *Doctrines of Salvation* 2:41, (emphasis his).
[10]Ibid. 2:67, (emphasis his).
[11]Kimball, *The Miracle of Forgiveness*, p. 243–244. On page 50 of *The Teachings of Spencer W. Kimball*, he added that a person "will never advance from his assigned glory to another glory. That is eternal!"
[12]Joseph Fielding Smith, *Man: His Origin and Destiny*, p. 532, (emphasis his).

For the sake of argument, suppose everyone in a given family was able to meet the requirements for entry into the celestial kingdom. The question now becomes: If every person is promised his own individual kingdom or planet, how will all members of the family be together? In other words, if the children were to reside with their parents on their parents' planet, it would appear to be impossible to exist on their own planets with their children. If a son-in-law won the right to his own kingdom, surely he would have to take with him the daughter of another family. Surprisingly, very few Mormons have seriously considered the illogical implication such an idea presents.

While the Bible does speak of believers being together in heaven, it certainly does not talk about heaven as Mormon doctrine presents it. Although few details are given, the Bible does say that it will be through Christ that all believers sit *together* in heavenly places, "that in the ages to come He might show the exceeding riches of His grace in His kindness towards us through Christ Jesus."[13] Revelation 19:1–6 states that in heaven "a great voice of much people" will be joined together to praise "the Lord God omnipotent."

While Mormonism depicts an eternity of self-made gods occupying themselves with procreation, the Bible speaks of the family of God, sinners cleansed through the blood of the lamb, exalting their God for ever and ever.

---

[13]Ephesians 2:6–7.

THIRTEEN

Do You Really Believe You Can Become a God?

Whereas Christianity has, throughout the centuries, defined salvation as synonymous with eternal life, Mormonism makes eternal life synonymous with becoming a god.

> Salvation in its true and full meaning is synonymous with exaltation or eternal life and consists in gaining an inheritance in the highest of the three heavens within the celestial kingdom. . . . This full salvation is obtained in and through the continuation of the family unit in eternity, and those who obtain it are gods.[1]

It is the goal of every faithful Latter-day Saint to aspire to a similar position which God himself now holds. In his 1844 sermon known as the King Follett Discourse, Joseph Smith declared:

> Here, then is eternal life—to know the only wise and true God; and you have got to learn how to be Gods yourselves, and to be kings and priests to God, the same as all Gods have done before you. . . .[2]

---

[1]McConkie, *Mormon Doctrine*, p. 670.
[2]Joseph Fielding Smith, *Teachings of the Prophet Joseph Smith*, p. 346.

Second LDS President Brigham Young stated:

The Lord created you and me for the purpose of becoming Gods like Himself . . . The Lord has organized mankind for the express purpose of increasing in that intelligence and truth, which is with God, until he is capable of creating worlds on worlds, and becoming Gods, even the sons of God.[3]

Mormon Apostle Bruce McConkie said:

Thus those who gain eternal life receive exaltation; they are sons of God, joint heirs with Christ, members of the Church of the Firstborn; they overcome all things, have all power, and receive the fullness of the Father. They are gods.[4]

Mormon Seventy Milton R. Hunter wrote:

No prophet of record gave more complete and forceful explanations of the doctrine that men may become Gods than did the American Prophet.[5]

If a person wants to have this doctrine fully explained, it seems odd there is really no one to turn to but Joseph Smith. If godhood was such a popular doctrine in the early church, why is it not emphasized in the Bible or, for that matter, the *Book of Mormon*?

One of the most often utilized LDS proof texts to support the notion that men can become gods is John 10:34. It was at the Feast of Dedication that the Lord once again confronted the religious leaders of His day. Verse 23 says that Jesus had walked into the temple and was near an area described as Solomon's Porch, or Solomon's Portico. There were four porticos surrounding the inner court of the Jews, which marked the barrier for the Gentiles. Signs made it clear that, should a Gentile pass the portico and enter the inner court, it would be upon pain of death.

It was here that Jesus again declared His divinity; for this He was accused of blasphemy, "making Himself God." In response to this charge, Jesus quoted Psalm 82:6 and asked the Jews, "Is it not written in your law, I said, Ye are gods?"

[3]*Journal of Discourses* 3:93.
[4]McConkie, *Mormon Doctrine*, p. 237.
[5]Milton R. Hunter, *The Gospel Through the Ages*, p. 115.

The Mormon interpretation of John 10:34 and Psalm 82 is faulty for a number of reasons. One, Jesus used the present verb tense ("ye *are* gods"). Not even the most faithful Mormon would claim to be a god right now. According to Mormon theology, the elevation to godhood comes in the next life.

Two, if it is true that Jesus was promising godhood in this verse, it would have been a travesty to call the men he addressed as being "God" material. Mormonism teaches that exaltation or godhood will only be accomplished when one is perfect and follows the law completely. If Jesus were speaking of obtaining divinity, He was certainly leading these unqualified men astray; these men did not even come close to meeting the strict requirements that Mormonism has set down for godhood.

Three, a look at Psalm 82, which Jesus quoted, reveals words of rebuke and condemnation. It is apparent that the Lord used this sacred writ to humiliate the self-righteous religious leaders. If this passage spoke of men who had obtained eternal life (or godhood), it would appear that eternal life is not very eternal since verse seven adds that these gods "will die like men."

Four, the passage in Psalm 82 refers to divinely appointed rulers or judges. The Hebrew word "Elohim" is used. This word is translated a number of different ways. Context is very important. Elohim can be translated "God," as in reference to the true and living God. It can also be translated "gods," as in false gods. Another way Elohim is translated is "judges." This is seen in Exodus 21:6 when speaking about a Hebrew servant who wished to remain with his master after serving for six years. The master was told to bring him before the judges (Elohim) in order to have the servant's ear pierced with an awl.

Elohim is also translated "judges" in Exodus 21:22 and Exodus 22:8, 9. The context makes it clear that human rulers are referred to in these instances. Perhaps the most troubling reference for the Mormon is to explain Mormon Apostle James Talmage's interpretation of John 10:34. He wrote:

> Divinely Appointed Judges Called "gods."—In Psalm 82:6, judges invested by divine authority are called "gods." To this scripture the Savior referred in His reply to the Jews in Solomon's Porch. . . . The inconsistency of calling human judges "gods," and of ascribing blasphemy to the Christ who called Himself the Son of

God, would have been apparent to the Jews but for their sin-darkened minds.[6]

Unfortunately, many Mormons are either ignorant of this quote or willfully overlook Talmage's correct interpretation.

Acquiring godhood is not unreasonable to Mormons since many LDS leaders have stated quite bluntly that God and man are of the same race. Mormon Apostle Parley Pratt stated:

> God's, angels, and men are all of the same species, one race, one great family, widely diffused among the planetary systems as colonies, kingdoms nations, etc.[7]

LDS Apostle John Widtsoe agreed with this thought. He said, "God and man are of the same race, differing only in their degrees of advancement."[8] It would be erroneous to assume this idea is no longer being promoted.

Some Mormons draw this conclusion from a phrase used by the apostle Paul in his address to the Athenians recorded in Acts 17:22–32. In his Mars Hill discourse, Paul quotes from a well-known poem known as the *Phenomena*. The poem, written by the Greek poet Aratus, speaks of mortal men as the offspring of Zeus, who depend on his goodness for their livelihood.[9] Aratus describes Zeus as one who takes care of mankind just as a father takes care of his literal offspring. Paul uses this illustration to introduce the true and living God of the Bible.

Some Latter-day Saints zero in on the word "offspring" and assume Paul is justifying the LDS concept that we are all the literal children of God, the result of a physical relationship between Elohim and one of his several heavenly wives.

Rather, Paul is doing nothing more than referring to a world view held by his audience and using some of those concepts as a preface to sharing the gospel. Christian scholar F. F. Bruce states:

> We are, then, the offspring of God, says Paul, not in any pantheistic sense but in the sense of the biblical doctrine of man, as beings created by God in his own image. There is indeed, a mighty

[6]Talmage, *Jesus the Christ*, p. 501.
[7]Parley P. Pratt, *Key to the Science of Theology*, 1978 reprint, p. 21.
[8]Hunter, *The Gospel Through the Ages*, p. 107.
[9]Robert Edwyn Bevan, *Later Greek Religion*, p. 35.

difference between this relation of men and women to God in the old creation and that redemptive relation which members of the new creation enjoy through faith as sons and daughters of God "in Christ Jesus" (Gal. 3:26). But Paul is dealing here with the responsibility of all human beings as creatures of God to give him the honor which is his due. And this honor is certainly not given if they envisage the divine nature in the form of plastic images.[10]

It would be difficult to assume Paul was justifying the idea that all mankind is of the same species as God. As Dr. Bruce points out by referring to Galatians 3:26, Paul rebuts the idea that all mankind is literally sired by God by teaching one *becomes* a child of God only by faith in Christ![11]

It would also be difficult to prove that Aratus believed or viewed himself as the literal offspring of God (Zeus). It is true that Zeus was believed to be a philanderous diety who fathered many gods and demigods; the mythology of the Greeks held that there were many "offspring" fathered by many other deities as well. While Greek mythology was subject to evolutionary change, it generally pointed to the god Prometheus, not Zeus, as the creator of mankind.

There does not seem to have been any canonical story of the creation of man in Greek mythology. There is a late tradition in Greek mythology that Prometheus made man out of clay, into which Athena breathed life and spirit . . .

The earlier Greeks seem simply to have supposed that men, like plants and animals, arose spontaneously from the earth.[12]

One version of the myth states that mankind was fashioned under the earth. When it came time to bring them into the light, Prometheus was given the task of equipping them with individual abilites.[13]

Historian Fritz Graf points out that man already existed before Zeus came into power:

Man was not created just to help the gods; he had dignity and,

---

[10]F. F. Bruce, *The Book of the Acts*, p. 340.
[11]See also Romans 8:14; 9:8. The *Book of Mormon* teaches this same concept in Ether 3:14 and Moroni 7:26.
[12]John Pinset, *Greek Mythology*, p.37.
[13]C. Kerényi, *The Gods and the Greeks*, p. 213.

in a sense, independence; accordingly, he existed already prior to the accession of Zeus.[14]

It was Paul's statement in Acts 17:25 that alludes to the image Aratus portrays in his poem. Paul described his God as one who gives life, breath, and all things to His creation. Aratus describes Zeus as one who tells when to plant and prune, and that he is the "great help of men."[15] In other words, while Mormons dwell on the word "offspring," Paul was emphasizing the providing nature of God.

Another verse commonly used by Mormons to support the idea that men can become gods is 1 John 3:2. Of this passage, Bruce McConkie says:

> Manifestly, if we emulate him so that his way of life becomes ours, we shall qualify for the same glory and exaltation that is his, for 'when he shall appear, we shall be like him.'[16]

By assuming that this passage refers to Mormons who will obtain the attributes of God, McConkie reads something into the passage that is not there.[17] This passage speaks about the Lord's Second Coming. Few Mormons would be so bold as to assume they will have obtained godhood at that time. Furthermore, far too many verses declare that God is unique and He alone is God.[18]

Lending even less credibility to the teaching that men can become gods is the way Mormon scholars turn to pagans, gnostics, and heretics to bolster this position. For instance, LDS Seventy Milton R. Hunter wrote:

> The Mystery Religions, pagan rivals of Christianity, taught emphatically the doctrine that "men may become Gods." Hermeticism, which had its rise in Egypt in the second or third centuries B.C., was a prominent religion in the Mediterranean world during the period of the rise of Christianity. Its literature, the *Corpus Hermeticum*, professes to be revelations to Hermes from his divine father and teacher. Hermes declared: "We must not shrink from

---

[14]Fritz Graf, *Greek Mythology*, p. 91.

[15]Bevan, *Later Greek Religion*, p. 35

[16]McConkie, *The Mortal Messiah* 1:18.

[17]McConkie's assumption is a clear case of eisegesis, or reading one's own meaning into a passage. The correct method of interpretation is exegesis, or allowing a passage to dictate its meaning.

[18]See Isaiah 43:10; 44:6, 8; 45:5–6, 14, 18, 21–22; 46:9.

saying that a man on earth is a mortal god, and that God in heaven is an immortal man." This thought very closely resembles the teachings of the Prophet Joseph Smith and of President Lorenzo Snow.[19]

Quoting gnostics doesn't carry much weight by the mere fact that these heretics were known for distorting the truth of the Gospel. Gnosticism emerged during the Apostolic Era and was countered through a number of New Testament and post-apostolic writings. In short, the gnostics believed that the supreme purpose of life was obtained through knowledge or "gnosis." Gnosticism denied the divinity of Christ and His redeeming work on the cross.

Some Mormons have even attempted to quote early Christian church fathers in order to support the idea that men may become Gods. This approach fails since many of those quoted by LDS scholars make it clear that they believed in only one God.[20] It would be logically incoherent for Christian church fathers to believe in one God, while at the same time believing men could be Gods as well.

Regardless of what an early church father may or may not have said, the authority of the Word of God is accepted by Christians over the teachings of any church father. Expecting a Christian to hold the teaching of a church father above that of the Bible is untenable from a Christian point of view. It is also inconsistent from an LDS point of view because Mormons themselves are very reluctant to accept many of the teachings espoused by their own leaders less than a century and a half ago.

Compared to the early Christian church fathers, there is much more available evidence to show exactly what Mormon leaders meant regarding certain teachings. Mormons who use the early church fathers as evidence for godhood, as they define it, use a double set of standards.

The Bible makes it clear that the relationship between the believer and his Creator is the same in both Old and New Testaments: He shall

---

[19]Hunter, *The Gospel Through the Ages*, p. 110.
[20]Christian apologist James White, in his review and rebuttal of *Offenders for a Word*, written by LDS authors Daniel C. Peterson and Stephen D. Ricks, notes that Tertullian, Hippolytus, Justin, Irenaus, Ignatius, Novatian, Cyril, Hilary, Augustine, John of Damascus, and even Origen all believed that there is only one God. *Pros Apologian*, Spring 1993.

be our God, and we shall be His people, not co-gods.[21]

When confronted with the LDS teaching that men can actually become Gods, some Mormons make excuses by saying they will be similar to, but not exactly like, God. Such a rationalization only works to undermine fifth LDS President Lorenzo Snow's oft-quoted couplet which states, "As man now is, God once was; as God now is, man may be." President Snow stated he had no doubt that this came by "direct revelation."[22] Bruce McConkie makes it clear that exalted humans will be like God in every respect:

> How can mortals become either gods or angels unless they obtain the same powers, the same attributes, and the same holiness that such eternal beings now possess? God is God and angels are angels because they possess the powers and perfections that now are theirs. If men gain these same states of glory and exaltation, can they do it without becoming like those who already have so inherited?[23]

While such an aspiration may satisfy the ego of many humans, it fails to account for the fact that God does not share the attributes held only by Him. His very nature is impossible to emulate. However, Spencer W. Kimball insists:

> To this end God created man to live in mortality and endowed him with the potential to perpetuate the race, to subdue the earth, to perfect himself and to become as God, omniscient and omnipotent.[24]

It is impossible for a finite human being to obtain omniscience, or the ability to know all things.[25] The Bible declares that God's omniscience covers not only the present and the past, but the future as well.[26] The Mormon who hopes to become all-knowing as God will

[21]Jeremiah 7:23; Revelation 21:3.
[22]Clyde J. Williams, compiler, *The Teachings of Lorenzo Snow*, p. 5.
[23]McConkie, *A New Witness to the Articles of Faith*, pp. 194–195.
[24]Kimball, *The Miracle of Forgiveness*, p. 2.
[25]The attribute of omniscience also causes a problem because the Mormon God is supposed to be an exalted being who at one time was a human with limited knowledge.
[26]Isaiah 42:9 says, "Behold, the former things are come to pass, and new things do I declare: before they spring forth I tell you of them."

apparently also have the ability to know the hearts of others.[27]

Because knowledge and events extend into infinity past and will extend into infinity future, it is impossible for a finite being to grasp it. It is impossible to attain infinite knowledge by the very fact that it is infinite! Dr. Francis J. Beckwith, a Christian philosopher at the University of Nevada, Las Vegas, gave the following illustration:

> Imagine that I planned to drive on Interstate 15 from my home in Las Vegas to Salt Lake City. The distance is 450 miles. All things being equal, I would eventually arrive in Salt Lake. But suppose the distance was not 450 miles, but an infinite number. The fact is that I would never arrive in Salt Lake, since it is by definition impossible to complete an infinite count. An "infinite" is, by definition, limitless.[28]

Consider also God's omnipotence. It is logically impossible for more than one being to have omnipotence since the word itself means "all powerful." It is impossible to have two all-powerful beings. To have omnipotence means to have more power than any other. The Mormon may try to escape this dilemma by claiming his God is not characterized by the attributes of omnipotence or omniscience. This would only confirm what evangelical Christians have been saying all along: the Mormon God is not the God of the Bible!

There is also the problem with who would receive worship. Jesus himself said that God alone is to be worshiped. When Satan tempted Jesus by requesting He worship at his feet, Jesus declared:

> Get thee hence, Satan: for it is written, Thou shalt worship the Lord thy God, and Him only shalt thou serve.[29]

Mormonism would interpret this to mean Elohim's children can only worship Elohim. It would have to be inclusive because there are supposedly millions of gods on millions of worlds who are being worshiped by their millions of offspring.[30] Since God is a "Being who has

---

[27]Ezekiel 11:5 reads, "I know the things that come into your mind, every one of them."

[28]"Philosophical Problems With the Mormon Concept of God," *Christian Research Journal*, Spring 1992, p. 28.

[29]Matthew 4:10.

[30]*Journal of Discourses* 7:333 quotes Brigham Young as saying, "How many Gods there are, I do not know. But there never was a time when there were not Gods and worlds. . . . It appears ridiculous to the world, under their darkened and erroneous traditions, that God has once been a finite being."

attained His exalted state by a path which now His children are per-mitted to follow,"[31] it would only make sense that the exalted Mormon male will receive worship from his children just as he now worships Elohim. Mormon Apostle Orson Pratt hinted to this when he said:

> As soon as each God has begotten many millions of male and female spirits, and His Heavenly inheritance becomes too small to comfortably accommodate his great family, he, in connection with his sons, organizes a new world, after a similar order to the one which we now inhabit, where he sends both the male and female spirits to inhabit tabernacle of flesh and bones. . . . The inhabi-tants of each world are required to reverence, adore, and worship their own personal father who dwells in the Heaven which they formerly inhabited.[32]

Because Mormons feel they are following the same path to godhood as their Heavenly Father did, it would seem obvious that LDS parents must also prepare to yield a child who will become a tempter. They must also have a firstborn son who will redeem their future offspring from the eventual sin that will befall them. Brigham Young made it clear that this is the pattern found on every world when he said:

> Consequently every earth has its redeemer, and every earth has its tempter; and every earth, and the people thereof, in their turn and time, receive all that we receive, and pass through all the or-deals that we are passing through.[33]

Such a notion is offensive to anyone who holds the Bible dear. Christianity has never defined eternal life as godhood; it has certainly never entertained the thought that Christians would receive worship since that honor belongs only to the Lord.

While many Latter-day Saints are working hard to prove them-selves worthy of eternal life, no one can really know if this position will ever become a reality, since obtaining it is dependent upon a person's individual righteousness. Joseph Fielding Smith, the tenth LDS president, explained that the requirements for godhood are very clear:

---

[31]Talmage, *The Articles of Faith*, 1982 ed., p. 430.
[32]Pratt, *The Seer*, p. 37.
[33]*Journal of Discourses* 14:71–72.

THE PRE-EXISTENCE OF MAN.

(*Continued.*)

23. The celestial beings who dwell in the Heaven from which we came, having been raised from the grave, in a former world, and having been filled with all the fulness of these eternal attributes, are called Gods, because the fulness of God dwells in each. Both the males and the females enjoy this fulness. The celestial vegetables and fruits which grow out of the soil of this redeemed Heaven, constitute the food of the Gods. This food differs from the food derived from the vegetables of a fallen world: the latter are converted into blood, which, circulating in the veins and arteries, produces flesh and bones of a mortal nature, having a constant tendency to decay: while the former, or celestial vegetables, are, when digested in the stomach, converted into a fluid, which, in its nature, is spiritual, and which, circulating in the veins and arteries of the celestial male and female, preserves their tabernacles from decay and death. Earthly vegetables form blood, and blood forms flesh and bones; celestial vegetables, when digested, form a spiritual fluid which gives immortality and eternal life to the organization in which it flows.

24. Fallen beings beget children whose bodies are constituted of flesh and bones, being formed out of the blood circulating in the veins of the parents. Celestial beings beget children, composed of the fluid which circulates in their veins, which is spiritual, therefore, their children must be spirits, and not flesh and bones. This is the origin of our spiritual organization in Heaven. The spirits of all mankind, destined for this earth, were begotten by a father, and born of a mother in Heaven, long anterior to the formation of this world. The personages of the father and mother of our spirits, had a beginning to their organization, but the fulness of truth (which is God) that dwells in them, had no beginning; being "from everlasting to everlasting." (Psalm 90 : 2.)

25. In the Heaven where our spirits were born, there are many Gods, each one of whom has his own wife or wives which were given to him previous to his redemption, while yet in his mortal state. Each God, through his wife or wives, raises up a numerous family of sons and daughters; indeed, there will be no end to the increase of his own children: for each father and mother will be in a condition to multiply forever and ever. As soon as each God has begotten many millions of male and female spirits, and his Heavenly inheritance becomes too small, to comfortably accommodate his great family, he, in connection with his sons, organizes a new world, after a similar order to the one which we now inhabit, where he sends both the male and female spirits to inhabit tabernacles of flesh and bones. Thus each God forms a world for the accommodation of his own sons and daughters who are sent forth in their times and seasons, and generations to be born into the same. The inhabitants of each world are required to reverence, adore, and worship their own personal father who dwells in the Heaven which they formerly inhabited.

26. When a world is redeemed from its fallen state, and made into a Heaven, all the animal creation are raised from the dead, and become celestial and immortal. The food of these animals is derived from the vegetables, growing on a celestial soil; consequently, it is not converted into blood, but into spirit which circulates in the veins of these animals; therefore, their offspring will be spiritual bodies, instead of flesh and bones. Thus the spirits of beasts, of fowls, and of all living creatures, are the offspring of the beasts, fowls and creatures which have been redeemed or raised from the dead, and which will multiply spirits, according to their respective species, forever and ever.

27. As these spiritual bodies, in all their varieties and species, become

Orson Pratt states that all exalted gods are to be worshipped by their sons and daughters. (*The Seer*, p. 37)

Unless a man can abide strictly in complete accord, he cannot enter there, and in the words of James, he is guilty of all. In other words if there is one divine law that he does not keep he is banned from participating in the kingdom, and figuratively guilty of all, since he is denied all. . . . So in the celestial kingdom, we must be worthy in every point, or we fail to receive the blessing. The kingdom of God must exist in absolute unity. Every law must be obeyed, and no member of the Church can have a place there unless he is in full accord.[34]

Such a requirement takes away one of the most precious benefits Christ gives the believer; that is, the assurance of salvation. In 1 John 5:13, the apostle John states that believers can know if they have eternal life:

These things have I written you that believe on the name of the Son of God; that ye may know that ye have eternal life, and that ye may believe on the name of the Son of God.

Because the hope of eternal salvation is based on the merits of Christ, Christians can rest assured that their salvation is secure in Him. It is only when a person feels salvation is based upon one's own personal works that this promise has no effect. For this reason, the Latter-day Saints cannot be absolutely sure where they will end up in the next life.

Why would John say we can know if we have eternal life if the assurance of eternal life was not possible?

---

[34]Joseph Fielding Smith, *Answers to Gospel Questions* 3:26–27.

FOURTEEN

Have You Ever Sinned the Same Sin Twice?

When it comes to the area of God's forgiveness, there is a vast difference between the God of Mormonism and the God of the Bible.

Because of the sinful nature that clothes all humans, everyone constantly struggles with sin and temptation. Not even the apostle Paul was exempt from the daily contentions with sin. Though he said that in his heart he delighted in the Law, he was constantly at war with the flesh:

> For that which I do I allow not: for what I would, that do I not; but what I hate, that do I.[1]

This daily grappling with sin makes it necessary to turn to God for His forgiveness. However, if Mormonism is true, no one can be assured that forgiveness is ever secure. *Doctrine and Covenants* 82:7 warns the reader:

> And now, verily I say unto you, I, the Lord, will not lay any sin to your charge; go your ways and sin no more; but unto that soul who sinneth shall the former sins return, saith the Lord your God.

[1]Romans 7:15.

125

Twelfth LDS President Spencer W. Kimball stated that the Lord anticipated the weakness of man, which would return him to his transgression, and therefore gave this revelation in warning.[2] The awful impact of *D & C 82:7* is clarified by Kimball under the subtitle *Forgiveness Canceled on Reversion to Sin.* He wrote:

> Old sins return, says the Lord in his modern revelations. Many people either do not know this or they conveniently forget it. "Go your ways and sin no more," the Lord warned. And again, ". . . Unto that soul who sinneth shall the former sins return, saith the Lord your God" (D & C 82:7). . . . Those who feel that they can sin and be forgiven and then return to sin and be forgiven again and again must straighten out their thinking. Each previously forgiven sin is added to the new one and the whole gets to be a heavy load.[3]

President Kimball quoted the words of Jesus spoken to the lame man at the pool of Bethesda and interpreted them to mean that his former sins would return if he sinned again. This is not likely. A close reading of John chapter five shows that nothing was said concerning this man's spiritual condition. Jesus merely recognized his physical condition and healed him. Later, Jesus again met this man and told him to sin no more (or more literally, do not continue in sin). Jesus knew this man's unreconciled position with God. His words to the healed man called for repentance lest a worse thing, eternal damnation, come upon him in the next life.

To assume Jesus was supporting the notion that forgiveness can be canceled completely ignores the many passages in the Bible that tell how God forgives the believer's sins and erases them from His memory. The God of the Bible promises that there will be no double indemnity, that a forgiven sin can never be used against a person twice. God declares:

> I, even I, am He that blotteth out thy transgressions for mine own sake, and will not remember thy sins,[4]

---

[2]Kimball, *The Miracle of Forgiveness*, p. 360.
[3]Ibid., pp. 169–170.
[4]Isaiah 43:25.

. . . for I will forgive their iniquity, and I will remember their sin no more.[5]

For I will be merciful to their unrighteousness, and their sins and their iniquities will I remember no more.[6]

In light of these passages, how can God bring back former sins upon a person if He refuses to remember them?

President Kimball proceeds to define "repentance that merits forgiveness." He states true repentance is when

the former transgressor must have reached a "point of no return," to sin wherein there is not merely a renunciation but also a deep abhorrence of the sin—where the sin becomes most distasteful to him and where the desire or urge to sin is cleared out of his life.[7]

Could President Kimball honestly say he cleared out of his life the very desire or urge to sin? While Christians should abhor sin, it is impossible for sinful humans to purge themselves of their very nature. The desire to sin is merely temptation. In and of itself, temptation is not sin. Rather, it is succumbing to the temptation that is sin. Speaking of Christ, the Bible states He "was in all points tempted like as we are, yet without sin."[8]

In a booklet published by the LDS Church, Kimball added:

The forsaking of sin must be a permanent one. *True repentance does not permit making the same mistake again . . .* Now the phrase "with all his heart" is vital. There can be no holding back. If the sinner neglects his tithing, misses his meetings, breaks the Sabbath, or fails in his prayers and other responsibilities, he is not completely repentant.[9]

Kimball added that "presently impure people can perfect themselves and become pure."[10] But the Bible says:

[5]Jeremiah 31:34.
[6]Hebrews 8:12.
[7]Kimball, *The Miracle of Forgiveness*, pp. 354–355.
[8]Hebrews 4:15.
[9]Kimball, *Repentance Brings Forgiveness*, pp. 7, 12, (emphasis ours).
[10]Kimball, *The Miracle of Forgiveness*, p. 355.

Who can say, I have made my heart clean, I am pure from my sin?[11]

The answer is obviously, "no one." All the good works in the world will not cleanse a sinner of his sins. If people could purify themselves, there would be no need for Jesus to pay the ultimate price for our transgressions. The only way to purify oneself is to have hope in the One who is pure, namely Christ Jesus.[12] It is faith in Jesus Christ and His cleansing power that purifies the sinner.

Kimball gave his readers a false hope that they could somehow be good enough to warrant a position in heaven. Honest seekers know this can never be because every person, on occasion, has sinful desires. While they may feel awful when it happens, they, like the apostle Paul, must fight their sinful nature constantly. If this is the case and Spencer Kimball was telling the truth, nobody has ever really been forgiven! The Mormon needs to realize the hopelessness of this dire situation. The struggle with sin will only be over when the person meets Jesus in heaven. Paul declared:

> Not as though I had already attained, either were already perfect. . . . For our conversation is in heaven; from whence also we look for the Saviour, the Lord Jesus Christ: Who shall change our vile body, that it may be fashioned like unto his glorious body, according to the working whereby he is able even to subdue all things unto himself.[13]

Comparing the natural body with the spiritual body, Paul wrote:

> So also is the resurrection of the dead. It is sown in corruption; it is raised in incorruption: It is sown in dishonour; it is raised in glory: it is sown in weakness; it is raised in power: It is sown a natural body; it is raised a spiritual body. . . .[14]

The Bible promises the assurance of forgiveness:

> In whom we have redemption through his blood, the forgiveness of sins, according to the riches of his grace.[15]

---

[11]Proverbs 20:9.
[12]1 John 3:3.
[13]Philippians 3:12, 20–21.
[14]1 Corinthians 15:42–44.
[15]Ephesians 1:7.

If we confess our sins, he is faithful and just to forgive us our sins, and to cleanse us from all unrighteousness.[16]

The mercy shown by God to Christian believers is that they are not given the just punishment they deserve for the sins they have committed or will commit. Romans 3:23 states, "For all have sinned, and come short of the glory of God." Romans 6:23 teaches that the "wages of sin is death; but the gift of God is eternal life through Jesus Christ our Lord." Without the acceptance of the gift of God through Jesus, a person's sins merit the punishment of eternal death.

If the God of Mormonism expects people to never have sinful thoughts, who could make it? It is obvious that the plan of salvation as proposed by the LDS leaders is different from the plan proposed by the God of the Bible.

---

[16]1 John 1:9.

FIFTEEN

Are You Keeping the Whole Law?

Emblazoned on the east wall of the Salt Lake City Temple (and other LDS temples as well) are the words "Holiness to the Lord." This passage, taken from Exodus 28:36, portrays the Latter-day Saints as a people who strive to live a moral code above that of others in the world today. While such a goal is truly commendable, the idea of righteous living can easily become distorted when its purpose is skewed and the requirements become unrealistic.

This was the case in ancient Israel. During the time of Christ, it was the religious leaders, specifically the Pharisees, who believed in a very strict moral code. Few dared to fault the spirituality of the Pharisee except, of course, the Lord Jesus. Unlike mortal men who often judge according to the outer appearance, Jesus had (and has) the ability to judge the heart. Because of this, He was not easily swayed by the flawed pharisaical view of piety.

In their zeal to appease a God whom they knew was holy, the Pharisees attempted to make their own set of rules as to how God could be pleased. Unfortunately this legalism surpassed the bounds of God's expectations for His creation and, in turn, robbed the people of the comfort and assurance their faith was supposed to give. Jesus ac-

131

cused them of laying burdens upon the shoulders of the people which they could not bear.[1]

Mormonism is very similar to the Phariseeism of ancient Israel. Salvation according to Mormonism is marred with requirements above and beyond those found within the pages of the Bible. While Jesus spoke of salvation as entering in by a narrow gate, the requirements added by the Mormon Church virtually close that gate shut.

Although many Mormons may understand that the "whole law" must be kept to reach this state of splendor, they may not realize how impossible this task is according to certain LDS leaders. This task is so difficult that even LDS leaders concede that many within the ranks of Mormonism, despite their sincere efforts, are probably going to fail. Noting that few Mormons can expect to become exalted to godhood, Joseph Fielding Smith, the tenth Mormon president, plainly stated:

> We are not going to be saved in the kingdom of God just because our names are on the records of the Church. . . . There will not be such an overwhelming number of the Latter-day Saints who will get there. . . . If we save one-half of the Latter-day Saints, that is, with an exaltation in the celestial kingdom of God, we will be doing well.[2]

According to Mormonism, heaven is made up of three levels: the celestial, terrestrial, and telestial kingdoms. Within the celestial kingdom are three levels.[3] Only those Mormons who reach the very top level will be able to become gods and goddesses. Eternal life is obtained by reaching the top level in the celestial kingdom. To obtain any level lower than this is considered damnation. Mormon Apostle Bruce McConkie describes eternal damnation as follows:

> Eternal damnation is the opposite of eternal life, and all those who do not gain eternal life, or exaltation in the highest heaven within the celestial kingdom, are partakers of eternal damnation. Their eternal condemnation is to have limitations imposed upon them so that they cannot progress to the state of godhood and gain a fulness of all things.[4]

---

[1]Matthew 23:4.
[2]Joseph Fielding Smith, *Doctrines of Salvation* 2:14–15.
[3]McConkie, *Mormon Doctrine*, p. 116.
[4]Ibid., p. 234.

In other words, those who do not obtain the highest level in the celestial kingdom will never become gods and will never be able to procreate with their goddess wives throughout eternity.

John Widtsoe, a former Mormon apostle, wrote that "men must do many things to win salvation in the kingdom of God."[5] This involves becoming perfect and obedient to the whole law.[6] Whereas the Bible declares it is Jesus Christ Himself who is the author and finisher of the Christian's faith, Mormonism makes man responsible for his own destiny. Consider these quotes from Joseph Fielding Smith:

> To enter the celestial and obtain exaltation it is necessary that the *whole law* be kept. . . .[7]

> But to be exalted one must keep the whole law. . . . Very gladly would the Lord give to everyone eternal life, but since that blessing can come only on merit—through the faithful performance of duty—only those who are worthy shall receive it.[8]

Reaching this state is tough for the Latter-day Saint since, according to former Apostle George Q. Cannon, Mormons

> . . . will be held to stricter accountability than any other people on the face of the earth. . . . We must be a pure people or we will be scourged; we must be a holy people or God's anger will be kindled against us.[9]

Cannon also taught that men are more accountable than women, putting a double burden on Mormon males.[10]

There are a number of requirements which must be obeyed in Mormonism for a person to become perfect and thus earn the right to exaltation. First, water baptism must be performed by proper (Mormon) administrators, and a succeeding baptism of the Holy Ghost. It, wrote McConkie, "is the initiatory ordinance into the Church on earth and the celestial kingdom in the world to come."[11]

As baptism opens the door to the celestial kingdom,

---

[5]Widtsoe, *Evidences and Reconciliations*, p. 75.
[6]Kimball, *The Miracle of Forgiveness*, p. 209.
[7]Joseph Fielding Smith, *The Way to Perfection*, p. 206, (italics his).
[8]Joseph Fielding Smith, *Doctrines of Salvation* 2:6.
[9]Cannon, *Gospel Truth*, p. 74.
[10]Ibid., p. 435.
[11]McConkie, *Mormon Doctrine*, p. 70.

celestial marriage is the gate to an exaltation in the highest heaven within the celestial world. . . . Only those who are sealed in the new and everlasting covenant of marriage and who thereafter keep the terms and conditions of that covenant will attain the highest of three heavens within the celestial kingdom.[12]

Celestial marriage equals temple marriage, agreed Seventy Milton R. Hunter. He wrote:

If men and women obey all the other laws of the Gospel except that of celestial marriage, they "are appointed angels in heaven, which angels are ministering servants, to minister for those who are worthy of a far more, and an exceeding, and an eternal weight of glory."[13]

Joseph Smith claimed that those who did not marry in the temple would never be able to have children in eternity. Procreation is an essential requirement to Mormonism's highest level of the celestial heaven. Widtsoe wrote:

Except a man and his wife enter into an everlasting covenant and be married for eternity . . . they will not have any children after the resurrection. But those who are married by the power and authority of the Priesthood in this life, and continue without committing the sin against the Holy Ghost, will continue to increase and have children in the celestial glory.[14]

Sixth LDS President Joseph F. Smith also stated:

Every man is a worse man in proportion as he is unfit for the married state. We hold that no man who is marriageable is fully living his religion who remains unmarried. He is doing a wrong to himself by retarding his progress, by narrowing his experiences, and to society by the undesirable example that he sets to others, as well as he, himself, being a dangerous factor in the community.[15]

Where in the Bible does it say that being single is to be an undesirable example that is even a danger to the community? Despair may be a reality for those who are married outside the temple or for single

---

[12]Ibid., pp. 118, 420.
[13]Hunter, *The Gospel Through the Ages*, pp. 119–120.
[14]*Teachings of the Prophet Joseph Smith*, pp. 300–301.
[15]Joseph Fielding Smith, *Gospel Doctrine*, 1977 ed., p. 275.

Mormons since they will be denied celestial glory.[16] Temple Mormons who divorce, except under certain conditions, can also lose their celestial glory.[17]

Another exaltation requirement is participation in the procreation process. Mormons feel it is their duty to provide human tabernacles for as many of God's spirit children waiting in the preexistence to be born here on earth.

Said Brigham Young:

> I have told you many times that there are multitudes of pure and holy spirits waiting to take tabernacles, now what is our duty?—to prepare tabernacles for them; to take a course that will not tend to drive those spirits into the families of the wicked, where they will be trained in wickedness, debauchery, and every species of crime. It is the duty of every righteous man and woman to prepare tabernacles for all the spirits they can. . . .[18]

Joseph F. Smith said that there is

> possibly no greater sin [which] could be committed by the people who have embraced this gospel than to prevent or to destroy life in the manner indicated . . . if we will obtain a fulness of joy, we must obey the law of our creation and the law by which we may obtain the consummation of our righteous hopes and desires—life eternal.[19]

Joseph Fielding Smith agreed, adding that those who practice birth control will inherit damnation. He wrote:

> Those who wilfully and maliciously design to break this important commandment shall be damned. They cannot have the Spirit of the Lord.[20]

Other duties that are essential to exaltation are temple activities such as the endowment ceremony and baptism for the dead, the neglect of which Joseph Smith said could cost a person his or her sal-

---

[16]*D & C* 131:2–3.
[17]Among others, see Joseph Fielding Smith, *Doctrines of Salvation* 2:81–82; Bruce R. McConkie, *Mormon Doctrine*, p. 118.
[18]*Journal of Discourses* 4:56.
[19]Joseph Fielding Smith, *Gospel Doctrine*, pp. 276–277.
[20]Joseph Fielding Smith, *Doctrines of Salvation* 2:89.

vation.[21] If all of the above requirements for exaltation were not enough, it is taught that only complete obedience brings eternal life. Joseph Fielding Smith said:

> Joseph Smith taught a plurality of gods, and that man by obeying the commandments of God and keeping the whole law will eventually reach the power and exaltation by which he also will become a god. . . . To be exalted one must keep the whole law. . . . Those who gain exaltation in the celestial kingdom are those who are members of the Church of the Firstborn; in other words, those who keep all the commandments of the Lord.[22]

He added, "To enter the *celestial* and obtain exaltation it is necessary that the *whole law be kept.*"[23]

It is possible that an otherwise worthy and honorable Mormon would not reach the godhood plateau by falling short on just one of the many celestial kingdom requirements. According to page 92 of the LDS Church manual entitled *Gospel Principles*,

> We must keep all our covenants with exactness. If we do, our Heavenly Father promises us that we will receive exaltation in the celestial kingdom.

The book also says that "now is the time to fulfill the requirements for exaltation."[24] It then proceeds to list eighteen "specific ordinances we must have received to be exalted." Following this list it reads, "In other words, each person must endure in faithfulness, keeping all the Lord's commandments until the end of his life on earth."[25] Again, only perfection will be sufficient. Joseph Fielding Smith states that even a cup of tea can bar a person from the celestial kingdom:

> Salvation and a Cup of Tea. You cannot neglect little things. "Oh, a cup of tea is such a little thing. It is so little; surely it doesn't amount to much; surely the Lord will forgive me if I drink a cup of tea." Yes, he will forgive you, because he is going to forgive every man who repents; but, my brethren, if you drink coffee or tea, or take tobacco, are you letting a cup of tea or a little tobacco stand

---

[21]Joseph Fielding Smith, *Teachings of the Prophet Joseph Smith*, p. 193.
[22]Smith, *Doctrines of Salvation* 1:98; 2:6, 41.
[23]Joseph Fielding Smith, *The Way to Perfection*, p. 206, (emphasis his).
[24]*Gospel Principles*, p. 291.
[25]Ibid., p. 292.

in the road and bar you from the celestial kingdom of God, where you might otherwise have received a fulness of glory?[26]

George Q. Cannon explained perfection in this way:

We, as a people and as individuals, should seek to attain to that perfection, to be as perfect in our sphere as God our Eternal Father is in His; and we cannot attain to that exaltation and glory which He has promised unto us unless we are thus perfect. . . .[27]

Twelfth Mormon President Spencer W. Kimball added:

Perfection is an attainable goal. . . . We will not be exalted, we shall not reach our destination, unless we are perfect, and now is the best time in the world to start toward perfection. I have little patience with persons who say, "Oh, nobody is perfect," the implication being: "So why try?" Of course no one is wholly perfect, but we find some who are a long way up the ladder.[28]

Lest anyone should misunderstand him, Kimball said:

I would emphasize that the teachings of Christ that we should become perfect were not mere rhetoric. He meant literally that it is the right of mankind to become like the Father and like the Son, having overcome human weaknesses and developed attributes of divinity. [Even though] many individuals do not fully use the capacity that is in them, [that] does nothing to negate the truth that they have the power to become Christlike. It is the man and woman who use the power who prove its existence; neglect cannot prove its absence.[29]

The Mormon who hopes to attain the celestial kingdom by his good works would be like an Olympian swimmer who would attempt to swim to Hawaii from the California coast. Although he might have the best of intentions, the fact remains that swimming from California to Hawaii is an impossible task. Although this champion swimmer might be able to swim closer to Hawaii than the average person, the natural laws of currents, fatigue, sharks, and an insurmountable distance would result in his falling short of his goal. In the same way,

---

[26]Joseph Fielding Smith, *Doctrines of Salvation* 2:16
[27]Cannon, *Gospel Truth*, p. 82.
[28]Kimball, *The Teachings of Spencer W. Kimball*, p. 165.
[29]Ibid., p. 26.

sin causes mankind to fall short of the glory of God, leading to death, no matter how good the intentions might be.[30]

In response, many Mormons may point to a passage such as Matthew 5:48, which says: "Be ye therefore perfect, even as your Father which is in heaven is perfect." To use this verse as interpreted by many Mormons is to only bring condemnation on oneself, unless the Mormon using the passage in this manner really feels he has reached perfection.

Mormons often overlook the key word "therefore" in this passage which refers to the preceding verses. The context speaks of a consistent love for our neighbors, whether friends or enemies. As explained by Christian scholar F. F. Bruce:

> God himself sets us an example in this regard. "Your Father who is in heaven . . . makes his sun rise on the evil and on the good, and sends rain on the just and on the unjust" (Matthew 5:45). He bestows his blessings without discrimination. The followers of Jesus are children of God, and they should manifest the family likeness by doing good to all, even to those who deserve the opposite. So, said Jesus, go the whole way in doing good, just as God does.[31]

Ignoring this explanation, a Mormon may attempt to explain how perfection does not necessarily happen in this lifetime but after death. Gerald N. Lund, a zone administrator in the LDS Church educational system, explains:

> But *perfect* can also mean "having all flaws and errors removed." A better question might be, "Do we have to be *perfected* to be exalted?" Here the scriptural answer is a resounding yes.[32]

If this is the case, then a verse such as Matthew 5:48 cannot be used because it is given in the present tense ("Be ye . . ."). Also, while this idea may be found in certain Mormon writings, by such authorities as Joseph Smith, Joseph F. Smith, and Bruce McConkie, this thought seems to confuse the issue. For instance, the *Book of Mormon* says:

---

[30]Romans 3:23; 6:23.
[31]F. F. Bruce, *The Hard Sayings of Jesus*, p. 75.
[32]*A Sure Foundation*, p. 205, (emphasis his).

For behold, this life is the time for men to prepare to meet God; yea, behold the day of this life is the day for men to perform their labors.[33]

While some Latter-day Saints may not feel that their works are essential for exaltation, there are many who do. One survey included in an 1984 LDS book showed what a group of Mormons believed must be done in order to reach the top level of Mormon heaven. James R. Cox listed the top 100 conditions as named by those in his survey including: exercise, plant a garden, read good books, sleep, control your thoughts, be humble, shop wisely, be out of debt, cease to be idle, paint house, fix yard, help Lamanites (the Indians), and even "become perfect."[34] The title of this book, *How to Qualify for the Celestial Kingdom Today*, speaks for itself.

If the average Mormon feels that each one of these (plus 87 more) legalistic rules are important for the celestial kingdom, then who could qualify? And what about future sin? In Mormonism, there is no room for error. A Mormon who hopes for exaltation must become more perfect. Sin undoes everything that had been accomplished previously. President Spencer W. Kimball described salvation as climbing a ladder. He said:

> Each command we obey sends us another rung up the ladder to perfected manhood and toward godhood; and every law disobeyed is a sliding toward the bottom where man merges into the brute world. Only he who obeys law is free.[35]

The Bible explains that the law was never meant to save anyone. Instead of a means to reach God, the law is a curse to mankind since it exposes his sin. Through His sacrifice, Christ redeems us from the curse of the law because He took upon himself the penalty for mankind's sin.[36] Following the law justifies no one:

> Knowing that a man is not justified by the works of the law, but by the faith of Jesus Christ, even we have believed in Jesus Christ, that we might be justified by the faith of Christ, and not by the

---

[33]Alma 34:32
[34]James R. Cox, *How to Qualify for the Celestial Kingdom Today*, Appendix A.
[35]Edward Kimball, editor, *The Teachings of Spencer W. Kimball*, p. 153.
[36]Galatians 3:13.

works of the law: for by the works of the law shall no flesh be justified.[37]

The apostle Paul understood completely that the Law was not designed to be, nor could it be, used as a set of rules that we must attempt to follow in order to gain salvation. The fact that we, as fallen sinners, have already broken God's Law makes that an impossibility. The Law is a tool devised by a loving God to expose the sinfulness of individuals in order that they might see themselves in their helpless state and rely totally on His mercy for salvation. As Paul reiterates, its purpose was to expose our sin, not to reveal our righteousness.[38] Paul emphasized the fact that it was Christ's complete obedience to the Law (not an individual's partial obedience) that makes the believer righteous. Writing to the church at Rome he said:

For as by one man's disobedience many were made sinners, so by the obedience of one shall many be made righteous.[39]

Most Mormons would quickly point out that they will inherit salvation based on their personal "righteousness." Notice Paul states it is the righteousness of one individual (Jesus Christ) that makes many righteous. Mormonism, in essence, places the responsibility of righteousness on the individual instead of recognizing Jesus who has already met the requirement of perfection. Because everyone has already disobeyed the Law, every person is worthy of condemnation. We have failed to be righteous and have no choice but to trust in what Christ already did for us by living a perfect life and paying the ultimate price for our sin by dying on the cross.

At this point it must be stated that the Bible never downplays holy living. God's people should lead exemplary lives and strive to be virtuous. However, good works come about as a result of experiencing God's saving power. Never does the Bible teach that good works are a requirement to receive salvation.

No matter how many good things we think we might have done, there is always a little more that we did not accomplish. Try as he or she may, the Mormon will never be able to satisfy the requirements of God. Just as it is impossible for the blood of sacrificed animals to take

---

[37]Galatians 2:16.
[38]Romans 7:7.
[39]Romans 5:19.

away our sins,[40] so too is it impossible to become perfect here on this earth, no matter how much good a person does. Only through Jesus' sacrifice on the cross can the sons and daughters of God be cleansed of all sin and, therefore, become "perfected for ever" in heaven.

> For by one offering he hath perfected for ever them that are sanctified.[41]

A Christian chorus sums up this concept:

> He paid a debt He did not owe;
> I owed a debt I could not pay;
> I needed someone to wash my sin away.
> And now I sing a brand new song:
> "Amazing Grace," all day long.
> Christ Jesus paid the debt
> That I could never pay.[42]

---

[40]Hebrews 10:4.
[41]Hebrews 10:14.
[42]Author unknown.

GLOSSARY

AARONIC PRIESTHOOD:

MORMON: One of two priesthoods. Known as the lesser priesthood (*Priesthood and Church Government*, p. 106). It is taught that Joseph Smith and Oliver Cowdery were visited by John the Baptist on the bank of the Susquehanna River on May 15, 1829; he laid hands on them and ordained them to the Aaronic Priesthood. The Mormon Aaronic Priesthood holds the *"keys of the ministering of angels, and of the gospel of repentance, and of baptism by immersion for the remission of sins"* (*Doctrine and Covenants* 13:1).

CHRISTIAN: Reserved only for those who were direct descendants of Aaron, the brother of Moses. Numbers 3:6–12 makes it clear that only those in the line of Aaron were to hold the Levitical Priesthood.

See MELCHIZEDEK PRIESTHOOD.

ADAM:

MORMON: Known in the pre-existence as Michael. Adam *"sat in the council of the gods in the planning of the creation of this earth"*

143

(*Mormon Doctrine*, p. 16). According to Joseph Smith, Adam participated in the creation of the earth and occupied a position of authority next to Jesus Christ (*Teachings of the Prophet Joseph Smith*, p. 158). Smith also taught Adam was the Ancient of Days, the father of all (*D & C* 27:11; 138:38). Second Mormon President Brigham Young taught that Adam was not created from the dust of this earth but rather from the dust of *an* earth (*Journal of Discourses* 3:319). He referred to Genesis 2:7 as one of many "*baby stories*" (*Journal of Discourses* 2:6).

CHRISTIAN: The first human created by God and formed "*of the dust of the ground*" (Genesis 2:7). It was through his disobedience in the Garden of Eden that sin entered into the world (Romans 5:12). The consequence of that sin was death. "*For the wages of sin is death . . .*" (Romans 6:23).

ADAM-GOD:

First taught openly by second President Brigham Young on April 9, 1852. Young claimed that Adam was Michael the Archangel, the Ancient of Days, and that Eve was "*one of his wives.*" He also said Adam "*is our Father and our God, and the only God with whom we have to do*" (*Journal of Discourses* 1:50). This teaching has been the source of much controversy and has since been denounced. In 1976, President Spencer Kimball referred to the Adam-God "*theory*" as false doctrine (*Church News*, October 9, 1976). Young claimed this to be a doctrine when he said, "*How much unbelief exists in the minds of the Latter-day Saints in regard to one particular doctrine which I revealed to them and which God revealed to me—namely that Adam is our father and God*" (*Deseret News* June 18, 1873, emphasis ours). Heber C. Kimball, first councilor to Brigham Young, concurred with Young's assessment when he said, "*The first man sent his own son to redeem the world*" (*Journal of Discourses* 4:1).

ADAM-ONDI-AHMAN (Adam-on-die-ah-mun):

Supposedly taken from the "*pure Adamic language*" and means the place or land of God where Adam dwelt. Mormonism teaches Adam-Ondi-Ahman was located in Daviess County, Missouri (*Mor-*

mon Doctrine, p. 20), showing that Adam lived on the North American continent.

AGENCY:

The ability to choose right from wrong, which goes back to man's pre-existence. *"Agency makes our life on earth a period of testing to see whether we are worthy to become like our Heavenly Father. . . . Without the gift of agency, we would have been unable to show our Heavenly Father whether we would do all that he commanded us"* (*Gospel Principles*, p. 19).

AGE OF ACCOUNTIBILITY:

The age of a child when he has *"sufficient mental, spiritual, and physical maturity to be held accountable before God for his acts"* (*Mormon Doctrine*, p. 852). Normally this is the age of eight (*D & C* 68:27).

ANCIENT OF DAYS:

MORMON: Adam. Joseph Smith stated, *"Daniel in his seventh chapter speaks of the Ancient of Days; he means the oldest man, our Father Adam, Michael"* (*Teachings of the Prophet Joseph Smith*, p. 157).

CHRISTIAN: One of the many names of God.

ANTI-MORMON:

A name usually attributed to "Bible Christians" who try to evangelize Mormons. Oftentimes Mormons accuse such people of being motivated by hatred and bigotry.

APOSTASY, TOTAL:

MORMON: True Christianity is said to have ceased after the death of Christ's apostles. This made it necessary for God to restore the *true church* through Joseph Smith in 1830. Without this belief, there is no reason for the Mormon Church to exist. The *History of the Church* declares, *"Nothing less than a complete apostasy from the Christian religion would warrant the establishment of the Church of Jesus Christ of Latter-day Saints"* (p. XL).

CHRISTIAN: Although the Bible mentions a time when *some* shall depart from the faith (1 Timothy 4:1) and that *many* shall be deceived (Matthew 24:11), it nowhere hints of a *total* apostasy. Jesus stated His Church would endure. Matthew 16:18 quotes our Lord as saying, *"I will build my church; and the gates of hell shall not prevail against it."*

APOSTATE:
An ex-member of the Mormon Church.

APOSTLE:
A member of the Council of the Twelve, the second level in the Mormon hierarchy. The twelve apostles are also known as the Traveling Presiding High Council and officiate under the direction of the First Presidency in all parts of the world.

ARTICLES OF FAITH, THE:
A list of thirteen fundamental and characteristic doctrines of the Mormon Church. Originally known as the Wentworth Letter, it was intended to briefly outline the basic tenets of the Mormon faith. *The Articles of Faith* is also a book written by Mormon Apostle James Talmage.

See WENTWORTH LETTER.

ATONEMENT:
MORMON: The sacrificial act of Christ, which nullified the spiritual and temporal death brought about by the fall of Adam. It allows mankind to be resurrected from the dead. This also paved the way for those who are obedient to "Gospel Law" to obtain eternal life through a life of good works. Mormonism emphasizes that it was in the Garden of Gethsemane where *"Jesus took on himself the sins of the world . . . in Gethsemane He descended below all things so that all could repent and come to Him"* (*Teachings of Ezra Taft Benson*, p. 14).

CHRISTIAN: Christ's sacrificial death on the cross (Philippians 2:8; Colossians 1:20, 2:14; Hebrews 9:22). The believer is reconciled by Christ's substitutionary death, which forgives sins past, present, and future. Christians are *"reconciled to God by the death of his Son, much more, being reconciled, we shall be saved by his life"* (Romans 5:10).

See *ETERNAL LIFE, EXALTATION, IMMORTALITY, SALVATION.*

AUTHORITIES:

See *GENERAL AUTHORITIES.*

BAPTISM, WATER:

MORMON: Baptism or immersion in water is synonymous with being born again. This ordinance is necessary if one is to be exalted. Only Mormons with proper priesthood authority can administer proper baptism.

CHRISTIAN: An act symbolizing the new birth, which is to be entered into after a profession of faith in Christ has been made (Acts 8:36, 37; 10:47, 48).

BAPTISM FOR THE DEAD:

MORMON: Also known as baptism by proxy or vicarious baptism, performed in Mormon temples. It is believed that the deceased for whom the ritual is performed will have an opportunity to receive the Mormon gospel in the spirit world.

CHRISTIAN: Although Paul mentions a practice known as baptism for the dead in 1 Corinthians 15:29, little is really known on the subject other than he appears to exclude himself from such a practice by using the word *they*. The Mormon interpretation is rejected as are all ideas of a "second chance salvation." Hebrews 9:27 clearly shows *"it is appointed unto men once to die, but after this the judgment."* This makes an after-death restitution with God an impossibility. Ironically, this same idea is taught in the *Book of Mormon* in Alma 34:34, 35.

BENSON, EZRA TAFT (1899-1994):

Became Mormonism's thirteenth president in 1985 following the death of Spencer W. Kimball.

BIBLE:

MORMON: One of the four standard works considered to be scripture. Of these, only the Bible is considered to be mistranslated and cannot be fully trusted. Article Eight of the *Articles of Faith* reads, *"We believe the Bible as far as it is translated correctly."* The King James Version is the official LDS Bible text.

CHRISTIAN: God's only revealed and written word, which is a complete guide to obtaining full salvation. Considered to be God-breathed and declared infallible (2 Timothy 3:16).

See INSPIRED VERSION, SCRIPTURE.

BIBLE CHRISTIAN:

See CHRISTIAN.

BISHOP:

Non-paid leader of a Mormon ward. His duties are similar to a Christian pastor.

See BISHOPRIC.

BISHOPRIC:

"Any office or position of major responsibility in the (LDS) Church, any office of overseership under the supervision of which important church business is administered." A ward bishopric consists of an individual ward's bishop and his two counselors, all of whom belong to the Melchizedek priesthood (*Mormon Doctrine*, p. 89).

See BISHOP, MELCHIZEDEK PRIESTHOOD, WARD.

BLOOD ATONEMENT:

MORMON: A doctrine that stems from the belief that the blood of Christ does not cleanse all sins; therefore, one who sins a sin beyond the cleansing power of Christ must atone for his own sins by having his blood shed. While current Mormon leaders may deny the blunt description of this practice as taught by their predecessors, tenth LDS President Joseph Fielding Smith wrote, *"man may commit certain grievous sins—according to his light and knowledge—that will place him beyond the reach of the atoning blood of Christ. If then he would be saved, he must make sacrifice of his own life to atone—so far as the power lies—for that sin, for the blood of Christ alone under certain circumstances will not avail. Joseph Smith taught that there were certain sins so griev-*

ous *that men may commit, that they place the transgressors beyond the power of the atonement of Christ. If these offenses are committed, then the blood of Christ will not cleanse them from their sins even though they repent"* (*Doctrines of Salvation* 1:135,138).

CHRISTIAN: It was Christ's death on the cross as the Great Sacrifice that provides cleansing for all mankind who place their trust in Him. The Bible maintains that the blood of Christ is powerful enough to cleanse from *all* sin. 1 John 1:9 reads, *"If we confess our sins he is faithful and just to forgive us our sins, and to cleanse us from all unrighteousness."*

See ATONEMENT.

BOOK OF ABRAHAM:

Included in the *Pearl of Great Price.* Joseph Smith claimed to translate the *Book of Abraham* from papyrus found on Egyptian mummies he purchased from Michael Chandler in 1835. Smith said the *"rolls contained the writings of Abraham"* (*History of the Church* 2:236). Later examination from qualified Egyptologists showed Smith was totally incorrect concerning his alleged translation. Despite this refutation, many Mormons insist the *Book of Abraham* is authentic and Joseph Smith a true prophet.

See PEARL OF GREAT PRICE.

BOOK OF COMMANDMENTS:

A collection of Joseph Smith's early revelations, printed in 1833. These were added to other revelations and renamed the *Doctrine and Covenants* in 1835.

See DOCTRINE AND COVENANTS.

BOOK OF MORMON:

One of Mormonism's standard works. It contains the story of a group of Jews led by a man named Lehi who left Israel and sailed to the American continent around 600 B.C. with, among others, his sons Nephi and Laman. The book records the wars and ultimate demise of their followers known as Nephites and Lamanites. The narrative also includes the story of a group of people known as the Jaredites whom God spared from having their language confused at the Tower of Babel. Joseph Smith claimed the *Book of Mormon* was *"the most correct of any book on earth, and the keystone of our religion, and a man would get nearer to God by abiding by its precepts, than by any other book"* (*Teachings of the Prophet Joseph Smith*, p .194).

See LAMANITES, NEPHITES, SEER STONE, SCRIPTURES.

BOOK OF MOSES:

Found in the *Pearl of Great Price*, one of Mormonism's standard works. Mormon scholars claim the *Book of Moses* was given to Joseph Smith by direct revelation in June of 1830. Its purpose was to restore many *"lost truths"* that are not included in the Pentateuch. Mormon Apostle Bruce McConkie claimed the *Book of Moses "is one of the most important documents the Lord has ever revealed"* (*Mormon Doctrine*, p. 564).

See PEARL OF GREAT PRICE.

BORN AGAIN:

MORMON: Baptism in water. *"The second birth begins when men are baptized in water by a legal administrator; it is completed when they actually receive the companionship of the Holy Ghost"* (*Mormon Doctrine*, p. 101).

CHRISTIAN: When a sinner places his faith in Christ, he becomes a child of God and is born again into the family of God. *"If any man be in Christ, he is a new creature; old things are passed away; behold, all things are become new"* (2 Corinthians 5:17).

See SALVATION.

BRANCH:

Mormon congregations that are not large enough or stable enough to form wards. These are divided into two categories: independent branches, which comprise larger and more powerful branches, and dependent branches, usually smaller in size and "less endowed" with local leadership. Several branches comprise a district.

See STAKE, WARD.

BRETHREN:

Mormons in general. It is also used to denote the Mormon leadership.

See GENERAL AUTHORITY.

BURNING IN THE BOSOM:

See TESTIMONY (MORMON).

BYU:

Brigham Young University. A college and graduate school located in Provo, Utah, owned by the Mormon Church. Extension campuses are located in Hawaii and Israel.

CELESTIAL KINGDOM:

The highest form of Mormon heaven gained only by complete obedience to the Mormon gospel (*Mormon Doctrine*, p. 116). There are three levels in the celestial kingdom, the highest being called the Church of the Firstborn.

See CHURCH OF THE FIRSTBORN.

CELESTIAL MARRIAGE:

Marriages performed in Mormon temples, which are not only binding in this life but also in the next. *Celestial* marriage and *plural* marriage (polygamy) meant the same thing in Mormonism's earlier years.

See POLYGAMY.

CHILD OF GOD:

MORMON: All humans are the literal children of God, born in the pre-existence as offspring of Heavenly Father and one of his heavenly wives.

CHRISTIAN: Sinners who have trusted in Christ for their salvation. Galatians 3:26 says, *"For ye are all the children of God by faith in Christ Jesus."*

CHRISTIAN:

MORMON: A member of the Mormon Church. *"Mormons are true Christians; their worship is the pure unadulterated Christianity authored by Christ and accepted by Peter, James, and John and all the ancient saints" (Mormon Doctrine,* p. 513).

CHRISTIAN: A true follower of Jesus Christ (John 6:47; Romans 10:9,10).

CHRISTIANITY:

MORMON: Mormonism. *"Christianity is found among the saints who have the fullness of the gospel, and a perverted Christianity holds sway among the so-called Christians of apostate Christendom" (Mormon Doctrine,* p. 132).

CHRISTIAN: Based on the teachings and practices of Jesus Christ and His apostles. Historically these teachings include the Trinitarian view of God, the Virgin Birth of Christ, authority of the Bible, vicarious atonement of Christ, His bodily resurrection, and His imminent return.

CHURCH, THE:

MORMON: The Mormon Church, officially known as the Church of Jesus Christ of Latter-day Saints. According to Mormonism, all other churches are in a state of apostasy. *Doctrine and Covenants* 1:30 describes the Mormon Church as *"the only true and living church upon the face of the whole earth."* Mormon Apostle Orson Pratt taught that ". . . *all other churches are entirely destitute of all authority from God; and any person who receives Baptism, or the Lord's supper from their hands will highly offend God; for he looks upon them as the most corrupt of all people" (The Seer,* p. 255). Because of this, Mormonism teaches membership in this church is the only way to be truly saved. Mormon Apostle Mark E. Peterson stated, *"Salvation is in the church [Mormon] and of the church, and is obtained only through the church" (Deseret News,* Church Section, April 14, 1973, p. 14).

CHRISTIAN: Composed of individuals who have recognized their sinfulness and have placed their faith in Jesus Christ as their Savior. It is not denominational buildings nor organizations that comprise the Church but rather God's people. Acts 4:12 reads, *"For there is none other name under heaven given among men, whereby we must be saved."* That *name* is Jesus Christ, not the

Mormon Church. The Apostle Paul makes it clear in 1 Corinthians 12:27 that we, as individual believers in Christ, are the Body of Christ. It says, *"Now ye are the body of Christ, and members in particular."*

CHURCH NEWS:
A weekly tabloid-size periodical reporting LDS Church news and events.

CHURCH OF THE FIRSTBORN:
The highest of three levels in the celestial kingdom. Only Mormons who keep all the commandments of God will enter this heaven and become Gods (or exalted) in eternity (*The Way to Perfection*, p. 206). *"Eternal life is life in the presence of the Father and the Son. Those who receive it become members of the "Church of the First-born" and are heirs as sons and daughters of God. They receive the fulness of blessings. They become like the Father and the Son and are joint-heirs with Jesus Christ"* (*Doctrines of Salvation* 2:9).

See ETERNAL LIFE, SALVATION.

COMPREHENSIVE HISTORY OF THE CHURCH:
A six-volume history of the Mormon Church compiled by Mormon historian Brigham H. Roberts.

CONFERENCE:
See GENERAL CONFERENCE.

COUNCIL OF FIFTY:
See DANITES.

COUNCIL IN HEAVEN:
A council of the gods held in the pre-existence to arrange for the creation and peopling of the earth. This council was called by Elohim, the *"head of the Gods"* (*Teachings of the Prophet Joseph Smith*, p. 349). Also present were Jehovah, Michael, and Lucifer. This council also determined how mankind would be saved.

See ADAM, ELOHIM, JEHOVAH, LUCIFER, PRE-EXISTENCE.

CREATION:
> MORMON: Joseph Smith taught that matter is eternal and God had no power to create out of nothing. God reorganized already present elements, which had no beginning or end and cannot be destroyed (*Teachings of the Prophet Joseph Smith*, pp. 350–352).

> CHRISTIAN: God created all things "ex-nihilo," or out of nothing.

CUMORAH:
> Traditionally the hill in upstate New York located south of the town of Palmyra. Moroni buried the golden plates in this hill and appeared to Joseph Smith fourteen centuries later to reveal their whereabouts. Mormon scholars today are divided on the actual location of the Hill Cumorah. Many believe the hill was located in Central America.

> *See GOLDEN PLATES, MORONI.*

DANITES:
> A title attributed to Samson Avard, a Mormon who described the Danites as a band of armed men formed into companies of tens and fifties who were bound by secret oaths never to discuss their activities against those unfriendly to the Mormon cause. Mormon historians and leaders have since tried to distance themselves from this unpopular organization, which was also known as the Destroying Angels. In October 1838, Joseph Smith claimed that this illegal group had nothing to do with a Church-ordained Council of Fifty, which was set up as a defense mechanism against mob attack (*DHC* 3:178–182). Joseph Smith later denied that the Danites ever existed (*DHC* 6:165).

DEACON:
> MORMON: Chosen from among 12- to 14-year-old boys. His job is to "*watch over the Church and to be a standing minister to the Church*" (*Priesthood and Church Government*, pp. 164–165).

> CHRISTIAN: Men chosen as subordinate officers in the church. Their qualifications include not being greedy, being sound in the faith, and able to rule their children and houses well. They are also to be the husband of one wife (1 Timothy 3:8–12).

DESERET:
According to Ether 2:3 in the *Book of Mormon*, Deseret means honey bee. It was also the name given to the territory settled by the Mormon pioneers in the late 1840s. It was changed to "Utah" when the Deseret Territory became a state in 1896.

DESTROYING ANGELS:
See DANITES.

DOCTRINE AND COVENANTS:
One of Mormonism's standard works. Also known as the *D & C*. Printed in 1835, the *D & C* is primarily a collection of supposed revelations given to Joseph Smith by God. Parts of the *D & C* were printed in 1833 under the title *Book of Commandments*.
See BOOK OF COMMANDMENTS, SCRIPTURE.

DOCTRINES OF SALVATION:
A three-volume set of doctrinal writings authored by tenth LDS President Joseph Fielding Smith. Compiled in 1954, the jacket of this set reads, *"His [Smith] teachings are the Doctrines of Salvation as they have been made known by revelation. He is universally esteemed as the chief doctrinal authority of the Church."*

DOCUMENTARY HISTORY OF THE CHURCH:
Also known as the *History of the Church* or *DHC*. A seven-volume set expounding on the history of the Mormon Church.

ELDER:
The lowest ordained office of the Mormon Melchizedek Priesthood (*Priesthood and Church Government*, p. 111). By this office Mormons feel they have the authority to teach, expound, exhort, baptize, and watch over the church, etc. Also known as a standing home minister.

ELDER BROTHER:
Jesus Christ. Mormonism teaches that Jesus was the firstborn to Heavenly Father and Heavenly Mother. Since all humans are God's

literal offspring, He is by birth *Elder Brother.*

See JESUS CHRIST.

ELOHIM:

MORMON: God the Father. The literal father of Jesus Christ. *"Elohim is literally the Father of the spirit of Jesus Christ and also of the body in which Jesus Christ performed His mission in the flesh . . ."* (*The Articles of Faith*, pp. 466–467). Elohim was once a mortal man who progressed to the level of God. In the words of Mormon Apostle James Talmage, Elohim is a *"Being who has attained His exalted state"* (Ibid., p. 430).

CHRISTIAN: One of many names for God.

ENDOWMENTS:

"Certain special, spiritual blessings given worthy and faithful saints in the temples are called endowments, because in and through them the recipients are endowed with power from on high" (*Mormon Doctrine*, pp. 226–227). In order to enter the celestial kingdom and become a God, it is necessary for a Mormon to participate in the endowment ceremony. These ordinances are administered for both the living and the dead. Those who participate must swear to never reveal what they have learned in the ceremony. The endowment ceremony includes a film depicting the Mormon view of the creation and fall of man, the great apostasy of Christianity, the restoration of the gospel *"with all its ancient powers and privileges,"* as well as the absolute conditions of personal purity and strict compliance with Mormonism's requirements.

ENSIGN:

A monthly magazine published by the LDS Church covering Mormon news, events, and doctrinal and policy issues.

ETERNAL DAMNATION:

MORMON: Any eternal destination less than godhood. *"Those who do not gain eternal life, or exaltation in the highest heaven within the celestial kingdom, are partakers of eternal damnation"* (*Mormon Doctrine*, p. 234).

CHRISTIAN: Described in the Bible as eternal torment by fire and flames, which will occur to all who reject Christ. Revelation 20:15 states, *"And whosoever was not found written in the book of life was cast into the lake of fire."* Complete separation from God.

ETERNAL INCREASE:

The ability to procreate throughout eternity. This is reserved for temple Mormons who hope to gain eternal life or exaltation. *"Those who are married by the power and authority of the priesthood in this life, and continue without committing the sin against the Holy Ghost, will continue to increase and have children in the celestial glory"* (*Teachings of the Prophet Joseph Smith*, p. 301).

See *ETERNAL LIFE, EXALTATION.*

ETERNAL LIFE:

MORMON: Being exalted to the level of God. *"Only those who obey the fulness of the gospel law will inherit eternal life . . . Thus those who gain eternal life receive exaltation; they are sons of God, joint heirs with Christ, members of the Church of the First-born; they overcome all things, have all power, and receive the fulness of the Father. They are gods"* (*Mormon Doctrine*, p. 237).

CHRISTIAN: Described in the New Testament as living eternally with God in heaven. Also referred to as everlasting life. Eternal life is obtained when one places his faith in the Jesus Christ of the Bible. Jesus said, *"For God so loved the world that he gave his only begotten Son, that whosoever believeth in him should not perish, but have everlasting life"* (John 3:16). John the Baptist concurred when he said, *"He that believeth on the Son hath everlasting life: and he that believeth not the Son shall not see life; but the wrath of God abideth on him"* (John 3:36). First John 5:11,12 adds, *"And this is the record, that God hath given to us eternal life, and this life is in his Son. He that hath the Son hath life; and he that hath not the Son of God hath not life."*

See *SALVATION.*

ETERNAL PROGRESSION:

The progress of man beginning in the pre-existence and moving on to mortality and ultimately godhood. It began in eternity past and continues on in eternity future. Eternal progression involves the progress of God as well as man. *"We believe in a God who is Himself progressive, whose majesty is intelligence; whose perfection consists in eternal advancement—a Being who has attained His exalted state by a path which now His children are permitted to follow . . ."* (Articles of Faith, p. 430).

See PRE-EXISTENCE.

EVE:

    MORMON: One of Adam's plural wives. When Adam came into the Garden of Eden, he *"brought Eve, one of his wives with him"* (Brigham Young, *Journal of Discourses* 1:50).

    CHRISTIAN: The woman given by God to Adam in the Garden of Eden. Her name means literally the mother of all living.

EXALTATION:

    MORMON: Synonymous with eternal life or godhood. Faithful Latter-day Saints can become Gods who will be married throughout eternity and people their own kingdoms.

    CHRISTIAN: Living and reigning with Christ. 1 Peter 5:6 says that believers will be exalted in due time. Revelation 22:5 reads, *"..and they shall reign for ever and ever."* The Bible does not separate salvation from exaltation.

See ETERNAL LIFE, SALVATION.

EXCOMMUNICATION:

    A process by which an LDS membership is terminated. *" . . . Unless the excommunicated person repents and gains his church status again, he cannot be saved in the celestial kingdom. . . . Apostasy, rebellion, cruelty to wives and children, immorality, and all crimes involving moral turpitude, are among those which warrant excommunication"* (Mormon Doctrine, p. 258).

FALSE PROPHET:

    MORMON: Anyone claiming to be a prophet who does not belong to the Mormon Church. *"In this day and age true prophets will* be members of the Church of Jesus Christ of Latter-day Saints" (*Mormon Doctrine*, p. 608).

CHRISTIAN: Deuteronomy 18:20–22 gives two characteristics to look for in false prophets: (1) An inaccurate view of God or the introduction of other gods. (2) Inaccurate predictions concerning future events. Joseph Smith's prophetical statements show he met both qualifications of a false prophet.

FALL OF ADAM:

MORMON: Adam's transgression, which is considered to be a positive act. Mormonism teaches that mankind would not be able to procreate without the fall of Adam. *"Adam fell that men might be"* (2 Nephi 2:25). Adam's fall is considered to be a transgression, not sin.

CHRISTIAN: The result of sin against God's command to not eat the fruit of the Tree of Knowledge. Adam's disobedience caused death to enter the world. *"Wherefore, as by one man sin entered into the world, and death by sin; and so death passed upon all men, for that all have sinned"* (Romans 5:12).

See SIN, TRANSGRESSION.

FAST OFFERING:

An offering given at a fast and testimony meeting, which is designated to the poor. These funds are derived from money which would have been spent on a meal or meals.

See TESTIMONY MEETING.

FIRST ESTATE:

See PRE-EXISTENCE.

FIRST PRESIDENCY:

Consists of the Prophet/President and his two counselors.

See PRESIDENT.

FREE AGENCY:

See AGENCY.

GARDEN OF EDEN:
MORMON: Once located in the central part of the United States. *"The early brethren of this dispensation taught that the Garden of Eden was located in what is known to us as the land of Zion, an area for which Jackson County, Missouri is the center place"* (*Mormon Doctrine*, p. 20).

CHRISTIAN: It is generally believed the Garden was located in the easternmost end of the Fertile Crescent near the Persian Gulf.

GARMENTS OF THE HOLY PRIESTHOOD:
Sacred underwear worn by faithful temple Mormons which, they are told in the temple, *"will be a shield and protection to you against the power of the destroyer until you have finished your work here on earth."* Sewn into the garments are markings that resemble the compass, square, and level of Freemasonry. Mormons are told these garments are symbolic of the covering God gave Adam and Eve after their fall.

See *FALL OF ADAM.*

GENEALOGY:
MORMON: Researching one's family history for the purpose of performing temple work on behalf of the dead.

CHRISTIAN: Although researching family trees as a hobby is not condemned in the Bible, genealogical work as a part of religious practice is prohibited. *"Neither give heed to fables and endless genealogies, which minister questions, rather than godly edifying which is in faith"* (1 Timothy 1:4).

GENERAL AUTHORITIES:
Members of one of three governing bodies in the Mormon Church. These include: The First Presidency, which is composed of the Prophet/President and two counselors; The Council of the Twelve or Twelve Apostles; and the Quorum of the Seventy. Can also refer to one of a number of LDS leaders on the local level.

GENERAL CONFERENCE:
Held in Salt Lake City every April and October. A meeting where Mormons gather to hear General Authorities and lesser church leaders expound on Mormon teachings.

GENTILE:
MORMON: Basically non-Mormons.

CHRISTIAN: Non-Jews.

GOD THE FATHER:
See ELOHIM, HEAVENLY FATHER.

GOLDEN CONTACT:
A person who knows little or nothing about Mormonism but is eager to learn and may possibly join the LDS Church.

GOLDEN PLATES:
An historical record of American peoples written on plates of gold. In A.D. 421, Moroni, a Nephite warrior and son of Mormon, buried the plates in the Hill Cumorah. In 1823, as a resurrected being, Moroni revealed the whereabouts of the plates to Joseph Smith who was permitted to retrieve them in 1827. The *Book of Mormon* was supposedly translated from these plates. They were returned to Moroni and taken to heaven following the translation. It is believed by Mormons that the plates will be returned one day.

See BOOK OF MORMON, CUMORAH, JAREDITES, LAMANITES, MORMON, MORONI, NEPHITES.

GOSPEL:
MORMON: *"The gospel of Jesus Christ is the plan of salvation. It embraces all of the laws, principles, doctrines, rites, ordinances, acts, powers, authorities, and keys necessary to save and exalt men in the highest heaven hereafter"* (Mormon Doctrine, p. 331).

CHRISTIAN: *"Moreover, brethren, I declare unto you the gospel which I preached unto you . . . how that Christ died for our sins according to the scriptures; and that he was buried, and that he rose again the third day according to the scriptures"* (1 Corinthians 15:1–4).

GRACE:

See SALVATION.

GRACER:

A slang expression used by Mormons to describe a Christian who believes in salvation by grace alone.

GRANT, HEBER J. (1856–1945):

Became Mormonism's seventh president in 1918 following the death of Joseph F. Smith.

HEAVEN:

See THREE DEGREES OF GLORY.

HEAVENLY FATHER:

MORMON: Also referred to as God the Father or Elohim, a created being who was originally a mortal man and became God at a certain point in time (*Gospel Through the Ages*, p. 104). God is the offspring of another god who was also once a man, ad infinitum (*The Seer*, p. 132). Heavenly Father is but one of many gods.

CHRISTIAN: Also referred to as God the Father who was God from all eternity to all eternity. He is self-existent and independent of any external cause. He always was God and always will be God. He alone is God and knows no others. Isaiah 44:8 says, *"Is there a God beside me? yea, there is no God; I know not any."*

See ELOHIM.

HEAVENLY MOTHER:

The wife of "Heavenly Father." Early Mormon leaders openly taught that Heavenly Father was a practicing polygamist making Heavenly Mother merely one wife among many (*The Seer*, p. 172). Mormon Apostle Bruce McConkie claimed the teaching of a Heavenly Mother is an *"unspoken Truth"* not mentioned in the standard works (*Mormon Doctrine*, p. 516).

HELL:

See ETERNAL DAMNATION.

HIGH PRIEST:

MORMON: An office within the Melchizedek Priesthood that operates within the direction of the presidency. In the Mormon Church there are many individual men who hold this office of authority.

CHRISTIAN: Only one man at a time held this office under the Old Covenant. Numbers 3:6–10 states only those of the lineage of Aaron could officiate in this capacity. Hebrews 4:14 states that Jesus Christ is now the great high priest and that this office does not transfer to another.

HISTORY OF THE CHURCH:

See DOCUMENTARY HISTORY OF THE CHURCH.

HOLY GHOST:

MORMON: Third member of the godhead sometimes described as the Holy Spirit and sometimes described as distinct from the Holy Spirit. Mormon Apostle John Widtsoe stated, *"The Holy Ghost, sometimes called the Comforter, is the third member of the Godhead, and is a personage, distinct from the Holy Spirit. As a personage, the Holy Ghost cannot any more than the Father and Son be everywhere present in person"* (*Evidences and Reconciliations*, pp. 76–77). The LDS *Bible Dictionary* claims the Holy Ghost is another name for the Holy Spirit (p. 704). Heber C. Kimball, first counselor to Brigham Young, taught, *"The Holy Ghost is a man; he is one of the sons of our Father and our God; and he is that man that stood next to Jesus Christ, just as I stand by brother Brigham"* (*Journal of Discourses* 5:179).

CHRISTIAN: Third person of the Trinity. Synonymous with Holy Spirit.

See HOLY SPIRIT.

HOLY SPIRIT:

MORMON: *"The agent, means, or influence by which the will, power, and intelligence of God, and the Godhead . . . may be transmitted through space"* (John Widtsoe, *Evidences and Reconciliations*, p. 76). Mormon Apostle Parley P. Pratt taught the Holy Spirit was a *"divine substance or fluid,"* which filled Jesus Christ (*Key to the Science of Theology*, 1855 edition, p. 29).

CHRISTIAN: The third person of the Trinity. Synonymous with Holy Ghost. The word "Spirit" comes from the Greek word *pneuma*, translated both *spirit* and *ghost* in the King James Version.

See HOLY GHOST.

HOME TEACHERS:

Male members of the LDS Church given the responsibility of visiting the home of each member once a month. Their job is to encourage members to grow spiritually through prayer, study, and performance of their church duties (*D & C* 20:42–54).

HUNTER, HOWARD (1907–   ):

Became Mormonism's 14th president in 1994 following the death of Ezra Taft Benson.

IMMORTALITY:

Living forever in the resurrected state. *"Now there is a difference between immortality and eternal life. Immortality is the gift to live forever. It comes to every creature"* (*Doctrines of Salvation* 2:9). Mormonism teaches that everything will become immortalized, including the earth (*D & C* 77:1; 88:16–26).

See ETERNAL LIFE.

INSPIRED VERSION:

Otherwise known as the *Joseph Smith Translation* (*JST*). According to *Doctrine and Covenants* 73, Smith was commanded by God to work on a new translation of the Bible. It is said this was accomplished by way of revelation. While Mormon leaders have argued that the translation was not finished, the *History of the Church* reports that Smith finished his translation of the Bible in 1833. In a personal letter dated July 2, 1833, Smith wrote, *"We this day finished the translating of the Scriptures, for which we returned gratitude to our Heavenly Father"* (*DHC* 1:368). The Inspired Version is really not a translation at all because Smith did not use ancient manuscripts in his rendition. He merely changed the King James Version of the Bible wherever he saw fit and even inserted a prophecy concerning his own birth in Genesis 50:33 (*JST*).

See BIBLE.

INSTITUTE OF RELIGION:
An LDS school offering college-level classes on various subjects of Mormonism.

INTELLIGENCES:
A term that has never been clearly defined by the LDS Church. Mentioned in the standard works only in Abraham 3:21–22, this word can refer to either the pre-existent spirit offspring of God or individual eternal entities that existed before the pre-existence. At one time every person existed as an intelligence. Joseph Smith stated, *"Man was also in the beginning with God. Intelligence, or the light of truth, was not created or made, neither indeed can be"* (*D & C* 93:29). Twelfth LDS President Spencer W. Kimball said, *"Our spirit matter was eternal and co-existent with God, but it was organized into spirit bodies by our Heavenly Father"* (*Miracle of Forgiveness*, p. 5). Former B.Y.U. professor W. Cleon Skousen added that if God *"should ever to do anything to violate the confidence or 'sense of justice' of these intelligences, they would promptly withdraw their support. . . . He would cease to be God. Our Heavenly Father can do only those things that the intelligences under Him are voluntarily willing to support Him in accomplishing"* (*The First 2000 Years*, pp. 355–356).

See BOOK OF ABRAHAM, PRE-EXISTENCE.

INVESTIGATOR:
A person taking the Mormon missionary lessons.

See MISSIONARY LESSONS.

JACK-MORMON:
A lukewarm Mormon who does not fully practice his faith.

JAREDITES:
A group of people who supposedly came to the Americas around 2247 B.C. The *Book of Mormon* details their exploits in the book of Ether.

JEHOVAH:

MORMON: The name given to the preincarnate Jesus, the son of Elohim. *"It is to be remembered that the Personage most generally designated in the Old Testament as God or the Lord, is He who in the mortal state was known as Jesus Christ, and in the ante-mortal state as Jehovah"* (Articles of Faith, pp. 465–466). In the Mormon temple endowment ceremony, Jehovah assists Michael, the preincarnate Adam, in the organization of the world.

CHRISTIAN: A hybrid word taken from the tetragrammaton YHWH. Vowels were added to these consonants to form the word *Yahweh*, another name for God. The King James Version of the Bible often renders Jehovah as Lord; in many verses the words *Jehovah* and *Elohim* (Lord God) are combined when speaking of the one true God (Deuteronomy 6:4; Psalm 100:3; Jeremiah 10:10).

See JESUS CHRIST.

JESUS CHRIST:

MORMON: One of three gods in the Mormon godhead. The spirit brother of Lucifer and elder brother of the human race, Jesus was the literal firstborn son to Heavenly Father and Heavenly Mother who became a God in the pre-existence without experiencing mortality. Known in the pre-existence as Jehovah.

CHRISTIAN: The second person of the Trinity. God manifest in the flesh (1 Timothy 3:16) and the creator of all things, including Lucifer (John 1:1–3; Colossians 1:16–17; Hebrews 1:1–2). Jesus stands in equal authority with the Father since He is the true God (Philippians 2:6).

See ATONEMENT, JEHOVAH, PRE-EXISTENCE, VIRGIN BIRTH.

JOSEPH SMITH TRANSLATION:

See INSPIRED VERSION.

JOURNAL OF DISCOURSES:

A twenty-six-volume set of books containing sermons from various Mormon leaders until 1886. These sermons have often been categorized by many Latter-day Saints as mere individual opinions of the speakers; however, many of these sermons are quoted in LDS Church manuals and conference messages. The introduction to volume one states that these volumes contain *"purity of doctrine, simplicity of style, and extensive amount of theological truth which they develop."*

KIMBALL, SPENCER W. (1895–1985):
Became Mormonism's twelfth president in 1973, following the death of Harold B. Lee.

KINGDOM OF GOD:
MORMON: Mormonism teaches a three-fold meaning for the Kingdom of God. The Kingdom of God on earth is the Mormon Church. The Kingdom of God in the millennium will be both an ecclesiastical and political kingdom ruled and governed by the LDS Church. Following the resurrection of mankind, the Kingdom of God is the celestial kingdom and does not include the terrestrial or telestial kingdoms (*Mormon Doctrine* pp. 415–417).

CHRISTIAN: Also known in Matthew's gospel as the kingdom of heaven. It is the idea of God's rule or reign whether in this world or the world to come.

KOLOB:
Described as a star or planet nearest to the residence of God. It is near Kolob where God resides and where all humans live until they take human form here on earth. Tenth Mormon President Joseph Fielding Smith wrote, *"He [Eternal Father] revealed to Abraham that his throne is near Kolob, the great governing star of our universe"* (*Man: His Origin and Destiny*, p. 537).

LAMANITES (LAY-MAN-ITES):
The followers of Laman, who is mentioned in the *Book of Mormon* as the eldest and wicked son of Lehi. 1 Nephi 12:23 states that after the Lamanites *"dwindled in unbelief they became a dark, and loathsome, and a filthy people, full of idleness and all manner of abominations."* The Lamanites annihilated the light-skinned Nephites at the battle at the Hill Cumorah. Mormonism teaches that the dark-skinned Lamanites are the ancestors of the

modern American Indians. Others mentioned in the *Book of Mormon* include: King Laman; Laman, one of Moroni's soldiers; a city and river of Laman.

See HILL CUMORAH, MORONI, NEPHITES.

LATTER-DAY REVELATION:
Also known as modern-day revelation. In a specific sense, revelation given to a Mormon prophet by which he guides the church.

LDS:
Short for Latter-day Saint(s).

See MORMON.

LEE, HAROLD B. (1899–1973):
Became Mormonism's eleventh president in 1972, following the death of Joseph Fielding Smith.

LEHI:
According to the *Book of Mormon*, Lehi was a righteous man who was told to flee Jerusalem before its destruction in 600 B.C. He led his family by boat to the American continent. Others mentioned in the *Book of Mormon* by this name include Lehi, the son of Zoram; Lehi, the Nephite commander; Lehi, the son of Helaman; and the city and land of Lehi.

LUCIFER:
MORMON: One of the literal sons of Elohim and Heavenly Mother. A spirit-brother of Jesus (*Teachings of Spencer W. Kimball*, p. 34). Lucifer was present at the council of the gods, which was called to determine how mankind would be saved. Lucifer's plan was rejected resulting in his rebelling against his father Elohim (*D & C* 29:36, *Book of Abraham* 3:27–28).

CHRISTIAN: A fallen angel whose rebellion against God caused him to be cast out of heaven (Luke 10:18). A created being brought into existence by Jesus Christ (John 1:1–3; Colossians 1:16; Hebrews 1:1–2).

See COUNCIL IN HEAVEN, ELOHIM, JESUS CHRIST.

MAN:

MORMON: All mankind was *"in the beginning with God"* (D & C 93:29). Joseph Smith taught *"the mind or intelligence which man possesses is co-equal with God himself. . . . There never was a time when there were not spirits; for they are co-equal with our Father in heaven"* (*Teachings of the Prophet Joseph Smith*, p. 353). When editing this sermon, Church historian B. H. Roberts said the word *co-equal* should read *co-eternal* and blames the discrepancy on the stenographer's reporting. Brigham Young stated, *"It is fully proved in all the revelations that God has ever given to mankind that they naturally love and admire righteousness, justice and truth more than they do evil"* (*Journal of Discourses* 9:305).

CHRISTIAN: Man had his beginning on the sixth day of creation. His disobedience in the Garden of Eden caused man to take on a sinful nature. Romans 3:11–18 describes man as one who is in rebellion against God. *"There is none that understandeth, there is none that seeketh after God. . . . Their throat is an open sepulchre. . . . Whose mouth is full of cursing. . . . Whose feet are swift to shed blood. . . . There is no fear of God before their eyes."* See SIN.

MANIFESTO:

A declaration signed by fourth LDS President Wilford Woodruff in 1890, officially abolishing the practice of polygamy. This was in response to allegations that Mormon leaders were still teaching and encouraging the practice of plural marriage. Woodruff claimed these charges were false and that the leaders were not *"teaching polygamy or plural marriage, nor permitting any person to enter into its practice."* Long after this promise was made, future presidents Joseph F. Smith and Heber J. Grant were arrested, tried, and convicted of unlawful co-habitation (polygamy). Early Mormon leaders taught the doctrine of polygamy could not be overturned as this was an essential step to godhood. Interestingly, Wilford Woodruff, who signed the Manifesto in 1890, made this statement in 1869: *"If we were to do away with polygamy, it would only be one feather in the bird, one ordinance in the Church and kingdom. Do away with that, then we must do away with prophets and Apostles, with revelation and the gifts and graces of the Gospel, and finally give up our religion altogether and turn sectarians . . ." (Journal of Discourses 13:166).*

See CELESTIAL MARRIAGE, POLYGAMY.

MELCHIZEDEK PRIESTHOOD:

MORMON: A special authority given to Mormon men eighteen years and older designed to enable them to gain exaltation in the highest heaven. It is taught that this priesthood was restored sometime between May 15, 1829 and April 6, 1830. Peter, James, and John appeared to both Joseph Smith and Oliver Cowdery in Susquehanna County, Pennsylvania, and bestowed the Melchizedek (also spelled Melchisedec) Priesthood to them. It is named after Melchizedek, King of Salem (Genesis 14:18). Mormonism teaches this priesthood was handed down originally to Adam who received it from God (*Priesthood and Church Government*, p. 109).

CHRISTIAN: Although Genesis 14:18 speaks of a priest of the most high God named Melchizedek, nowhere does the Bible mention a Melchizedek *Priesthood* per se. Hebrews 5:6 states that Christ is a priest forever after "*the order of Melchisedec*," not a Melchizedek priest as Mormonism implies. It is clear in Hebrews 7:24 that the priesthood held by Christ is unchangeable and does not transfer to another since He lives forever.

See AARONIC PRIESTHOOD.

McCONKIE, BRUCE R. (1915–1985):

Mormon apostle and scholar credited with many books including *Mormon Doctrine* and the *Messiah* series. Probably one of the most often-quoted modern Mormon scholars.

McKAY, DAVID O. (1873–1970):

Became Mormonism's ninth president in 1951 following the death of George Albert Smith.

MISSION:

A voluntary commitment on the part of a Mormon. Although a majority of the Mormon missionary force is composed of young males in their late teens, females and retired people also devote their time and service to the Mormon missionary program. Length of service lasts eighteen months for females to two years for males.

MISSIONARY LESSONS:
Otherwise known as the *Uniform System for Teaching the Gospel.* A series of six lessons given to investigators, which helps to explain Mormon doctrines.
See INVESTIGATOR.

MISSIONARY TRAINING CENTER:
Also known as the MTC. The first and primary MTC is located in Provo, Utah. It is here the Mormon missionary learns doctrine and procedure that will be used during his/her missionary service.

MODERN-DAY REVELATION:
See LATTER-DAY REVELATION.

MOLLY MORMON:
A Mormon female who aspires to be everything the Mormon Church expects a woman to be.

MORMON:
Claimed by Latter-day Saints to be an ancient Nephite prophet who abridged and compiled the records of his people known today as *The Book of Mormon.* Originally this was a derogatory term given to followers of Joseph Smith. Today it is a non-offensive nickname commonly used to describe either the Church of Jesus Christ of Latter-day Saints based in Salt Lake City, Utah, or its members.

MORONI (Ma-rone-eye):
Believed by Mormons to be the son of Mormon. Moroni supposedly buried the gold plates containing the record of the Nephite people and later revealed their location to Joseph Smith in 1823.
See MORMON, NEPHITES.

MOTHER GOD:
See HEAVENLY MOTHER.

NAUVOO (nah-voo):
Literally means "beautiful place." Originally known as Commerce, Illinois. This city became the headquarters of the Mormon Church until Joseph Smith's death in 1844.

NAUVOO EXPOSITOR, THE:
A newspaper published by enemies of Joseph Smith. Its only issue appeared on June 7, 1844 to uncover Joseph Smith's abuse of authority in both ecclesiastical and civil affairs (Smith was also mayor of Nauvoo) as well as expose his plural-wife system. Three days later, on June 10, Smith ordered its printing press destroyed.

NEGRO:
See SEED OF CAIN.

NEPHITES (nee-fites):
The followers of Nephi, a righteous son of Lehi. The Nephites are said to have been exterminated by the Lamanites at the battle at the Hill Cumorah. Others mentioned in the *Book of Mormon* include: Nephi, the son of Helaman; Nephi, the grandson of Helaman; Nephi, the son of Nephi the disciple; and the land and city of Nephi.

See HILL CUMORAH, LAMANITES, LEHI.

NEW JERUSALEM:
MORMON: A city to be built in Jackson County, Missouri. The *Book of Mormon* prophesies the coming forth of the New Jerusalem that *"should be built up upon this land"* (Ether 13:5). Joseph Smith claimed New Jerusalem would begin with the building of a temple and that the city would become a gathering place for God's *"covenant people"* (D & C 42:35–36). Neither the temple prophesied by Smith (D & C 84:1–4) nor the city was ever built. Smith attributed this failure to God's enemies (D & C 124:51). Another name for New Jerusalem was Zion.

CHRISTIAN: Mentioned in Revelation 3:12 as a city of God reserved for those who have "overcome" earthly trials. Revelation 21:2 describes the New Jerusalem as a holy city prepared for the bride of

Christ. This city will come into play only after the former heaven and earth are passed away.

See ZION.

ORDINANCES:
Otherwise known as rites and ceremonies. *"Most of these rites and ceremonies, as illustrated by baptism and celestial marriage, are essential to salvation and exaltation in the kingdom of God"* (*Mormon Doctrine*, p. 549).

See ENDOWMENTS, BAPTISM FOR THE DEAD, CELESTIAL MARRIAGE, WASHING, AND ANOINTING.

PATRIARCHAL BLESSING:
A blessing or conditional prophetic utterance given to a Mormon either by a *natural* patriarch such as a father or grandfather, or an *ordained* patriarch appointed by the LDS Church to give such blessings (*Doctrines of Salvation* 3:169–172). *"We can learn more about our talents and calling when we receive our patriarchal blessings"* (Harold B. Lee, *Gospel Principles*, p. 10).

PEARL OF GREAT PRICE, THE:
One of Mormonism's standard works. This volume contains the *Book of Abraham*, the *Book of Moses*, and Joseph Smith's personal testimony.

PEEPSTONES:
See SEER STONE, URIM AND THUMMIM.

POLYGAMY:
Otherwise referred to as plural marriage. It was also known as celestial marriage in the early Mormon Church. Joseph Smith claimed God gave him this doctrine in 1843. Early Mormon leaders taught polygamy was essential if a man hoped to become a god. Brigham Young taught in 1866, *"The only men who become gods, even the sons of God, are those who enter into polygamy"* (*Journal of Discourses* 11:269). The practice of polygamy today is denounced by the LDS Church.

See CELESTIAL MARRIAGE.

PRE-EXISTENCE:

Also referred to as the *First Estate* or *Pre-Mortal State.* Mormonism teaches all humans lived near a planet called Kolob as God's *spirit children* before coming to earth and taking on human form. Since God's children could only progress so far in the pre-existence, it was necessary that they go through a probationary state here on earth in order to prove their worthiness to return to God's presence (*Gospel Principles*, p. 11).

See SECOND ESTATE.

PRE-MORTAL STATE:

See PRE-EXISTENCE.

PRESIDENT:

The highest office in the Mormon Church. It is the president's duty to preside over the whole church. Also known as the Prophet, Seer, and Revelator, he is chosen from among the Council of the Twelve Apostles. Revelations concerning the LDS Church must come through the Presidency.

PRIESTHOOD:

See AARONIC AND MELCHIZEDEK PRIESTHOOD.

PROPHET:

See PRESIDENT.

QUAD:

The Bible, *Book of Mormon, Doctrine and Covenants,* and *Pearl of Great Price* bound together as one book.

QUETZALCOATL:

An ancient Central American Aztec god believed by many Mormons to be Jesus Christ who visited the Americas after His resurrection. The name means *plumed serpent* and is derived from a colorful bird (quetzal) and a snake (coatl). Many Mormon scholars have debunked the theory connecting Quetzalcoatl with Christ.

RECOMMEND:

See TEMPLE RECOMMEND.

REFORMATION:

MORMON: A moral and spiritual awakening that began in Utah in 1856.

CHRISTIAN: A sixteenth-century movement within Christianity to return to the basics of the faith as laid down in the Bible.

REFORMED EGYPTIAN:

Mormon 9:32 describes the characters written upon the gold plates containing the *Book of Mormon* to be in a language called Reformed Egyptian. It should be noted that there is no evidence to show this language ever existed.

RM:

Short for Returned Missionary (Mormon).

See MISSION.

REORGANIZED CHURCH OF JESUS CHRIST OF LATTER-DAY SAINTS:

Otherwise known as the RLDS. It is the second largest splinter group of the Latter-day Saint movement. Headquartered in Independence, Missouri, this group historically has been led by direct descendants of Joseph Smith, whereas the Utah Mormons take their leaders from the Quorum of the Twelve, or twelve Apostles. A comparison between RLDS and LDS teachings show the RLDS to be less controversial than their LDS counterparts. RLDS do not like being called Mormons.

RESTORATION:

The act by which God returned true Christianity to the earth. Mormonism teaches Christianity ceased to exist soon after the original twelve apostles died and that God restored the true church through Joseph Smith in 1830.

See APOSTASY.

SACRAMENT MEETING:

A solemn service held weekly, that allows Mormons to renew their covenants by partaking of the sacrament (bread and water).

SAINTS:

MORMON: Members of the Mormon Church.

CHRISTIAN: Those who have placed their faith in Jesus Christ. True believers are called saints.

SALVATION:

MORMON: Salvation is broken down into two categories. Individual or personal salvation (more correctly termed "exaltation") and general salvation. The road to individual salvation begins with a belief that Joseph Smith was a true prophet sent by God. Tenth President Joseph Fielding Smith stated that there is *"No Salvation Without Accepting Joseph Smith"* (*Doctrines of Salvation* 1:189). Exaltation requirements include living a life of good works and temple participation. Keeping the whole law is absolutely essential. *"Those who gain exaltation in the celestial kingdom are those who are members of the Church of the Firstborn; in other words, those who keep ALL of the commandments of the Lord"* (*Doctrines of Salvation* 2:41, emphasis his). General salvation, otherwise called salvation by grace, was obtained through the death of Christ and is nothing more than universal resurrection, which occurs to all people regardless of their beliefs or lifestyle.

CHRISTIAN: Salvation is only obtained by trusting Christ. A person must recognize himself as a sinner and trust in Christ alone to receive forgiveness of sins and eternal life. Salvation and exaltation are synonymous terms. Those who receive Christ as Savior will be resurrected unto eternal life while those who refuse will be resurrected to damnation (John 5:29) and be eternally separated from God. Trusting in the fact that Christ paid the complete penalty for man's sins warrants salvation. Jesus said, *"He that believeth on me hath everlasting life"* (John 6:47).

See EXALTATION.

SATAN:

See LUCIFER.

SCRIPTURE:

MORMON: The Bible, *The Book of Mormon*, the *Doctrine and Covenants*, and the *Pearl of Great Price*. Also called the standard works, these books are considered to be authoritative.

CHRISTIAN: Protestant Christianity has maintained that the only written authority for life and faith is the Bible, a collection of sixty-six books written over a period from about 1500 B.C. to the end of the first century A.D. This was accomplished by God, who inspired men of different backgrounds to record the history of God's people and the doctrines set forth by Him. The Bible is a completely sufficient guide to obtaining full salvation. 2 Timothy 3:16–17 reads, *"All scripture is given by inspiration of God, and is profitable for doctrine, for reproof, for correction, for instruction in righteousness: That the man of God may be perfect, thoroughly furnished unto all good works."*

See *BIBLE, BOOK OF MORMON, DOCTRINE AND COVENANTS, PEARL OF GREAT PRICE.*

SEALINGS:

An ordinance performed in Mormon temples that binds a man and wife as well as their children into a family unit that will be preserved throughout eternity. Sealing ordinances can also be performed by proxy on behalf of the dead.

See *ORDINANCES.*

SECOND ANOINTING:

A rare temple ordinance whereby a person has his or her *"calling and election made sure."* Only Mormons who have received the second anointing can know for sure in this life if they will obtain godhood upon death. Not much is known about the second anointing because of the secret nature of this ceremony.

SECOND ESTATE:

Mortality. Physical bodies were given to those who were faithful in the pre-existence, or first estate. Those who were unfaithful (the devil and his angels) were denied physical bodies and must forever remain as spirits.

See *PRE-EXISTENCE.*

SEED OF CAIN:
> Members of the black race (Moses 7:2). Until 1978, LDS leaders taught that *"one drop of negro blood"* could ban a Mormon male from holding the Mormon priesthood. The dark skin was the mark given to those pre-mortal spirits who were *"less valiant in pre-existence"* (*Mormon Doctrine*, p. 527) when Lucifer rebelled against God. These spirits came to earth through the lineage of Cain, the eldest son of Adam and Eve. Tenth LDS President Joseph Fielding Smith claimed, *"Cain became the father of an inferior race"* (*Way to Perfection*, p. 101).

SEER, THE:
> A Mormon periodical that was named in *"commemoration of Joseph Smith, the great Seer of the last days."* Edited by Mormon Apostle Orson Pratt, *The Seer* was to be *"occupied with original matter, illucidating (sic) the doctrines of the Church of Jesus Christ of Latter-day Saints, as revealed in both ancient and modern Revelations"* (January 1853, p. 1).

SEER STONE:
> Described as a chocolate-colored, egg-shaped rock Joseph Smith found while digging a well near Palmyra, New York (*Comprehensive History of the Church* 1:129). A number of witnesses claimed Smith used the stone when translating the *Book of Mormon*.
>
> See BOOK OF MORMON, URIM AND THUMMIM.

SEMINARY:
> MORMON: A junior-high or high-school level course that teaches the basics of the Mormon faith to young people.
>
> CHRISTIAN: A school or college offering training for those entering the ministry.

SEVENTY:
> Either a member of the First Quorum of the Seventy or the Second Quorum (organized in 1989). Otherwise known as traveling ministers, the Seventies act under direction of the twelve apostles.

SIN:

MORMON: Acts of transgression against revealed law. It is taught that man is by nature a lover of truth and righteousness. Brigham Young stated, *"It is, however, universally received by professors of religion as a Scriptural doctrine that man is naturally opposed to God. This is not so"* (JOD 9:305). Third Mormon President John Taylor said, *"In fact, as the President [Young] stated here not long ago, it is not natural for men to be evil"* (JOD 10:50). According to Mormon teaching, there are times when transgression is not considered a sin such as in the case of Adam in the Garden of Eden.

CHRISTIAN: Sin is synonymous with transgression. Sin permeates all of mankind; it is an innate part of man's nature. King Solomon wrote in Ecclesiastes 9:3, *"The heart of the sons of men is full of evil, and madness is in their heart while they live."* Psalm 14:2–3 says, *"The Lord looked down from heaven upon the children of men, to see if there were any that did understand, and seek after God. They are all gone aside, they are all together become filthy; there is none that doeth good, no, not one."* A man transgresses revealed law because he is by nature a transgressor. Just as a dog acts like a dog, so too, a sinner will act like a sinner. Upon faith in the true Jesus, a person is transformed into a new creature in Christ and is given the power to overcome sin (Romans 6:14).

SMITH, GEORGE ALBERT (1870–1951):

Became Mormonism's eighth president in 1945, following the death of Heber J. Grant.

SMITH, JR., JOSEPH (1805–1844):

Founded the Mormon Church in 1830 and became its first president. It was Joseph Smith who claimed he saw God the Father and Jesus Christ and was told that all Christian churches were an abomination in God's sight. Using magical seer stones called the Urim and the Thummim, Smith is said to have translated the *Book of Mormon* in 1830, using the Golden Plates left to him by the angel Moroni. He died in a gun battle in Carthage, Illinois, on June 27, 1844.

See BOOK OF MORMON, GOLDEN PLATES, MORONI, URIM AND THUMMIM.

SMITH, JOSEPH F. (1838–1919):
A nephew of Joseph Smith who became Mormonism's sixth president in 1901 following the death of Lorenzo Snow.

SMITH, JOSEPH FIELDING (1876–1972):
A son of Joseph F. Smith who became Mormonism's tenth president in 1970 following the death of David O. McKay.

See DOCTRINES OF SALVATION.

SNOW, LORENZO (1814–1901):
Became Mormonism's fifth president in 1898 following the death of Wilford Woodruff.

SONS OF PERDITION:
Those who rebelled with Lucifer in the pre-existence. The term can also apply to those in this life who had a perfect knowledge of Mormonism but chose to reject it and fight against it.

See PRE-EXISTENCE.

SPIRIT CHILDREN:
Refers to either the offspring of God in the pre-existence or the offspring that will be born to those Mormons who receive godhood in the celestial kingdom.

See ETERNAL INCREASE, PRE-EXISTENCE.

STAKE:
A geographical grouping within the Mormon Church, which consists of wards and branches. Groups of stakes are combined to form regions or districts.

See WARD.

STANDARD WORKS:
See SCRIPTURE.

STICK OF EPHRAIM:
MORMON: The *Book of Mormon.* Mormonism teaches that the word translated *stick* in Ezekiel 37:16 literally means a book or scroll and that Ezekiel was prophesying the coming of the *Book of Mormon.*

CHRISTIAN: A literal piece of wood used as an illustration in Ezekiel 37 to describe the northern kingdom of Israel. The prophecy foretold the reunification of two nations—Israel and Judah (Ezekiel 37:22).

STICK OF JUDAH:
MORMON: The Bible.

CHRISTIAN: Used as an illustration in Ezekiel 37 to describe the southern kingdom of Judah.

See STICK OF EPHRAIM.

SUNSTONE MORMON:
A slang expression describing a liberal Mormon. *Sunstone* is a magazine known for its more liberal (and sometimes more objective) view of Mormonism.

TAYLOR, JOHN (1808–1887):
Became Mormonism's third president following the death of Brigham Young.

TELESTIAL KINGDOM:
The lowest form of Mormon heaven reserved for the wicked of this world.

TEMPLE:
MORMON: Dozens of buildings scattered throughout the world where esoteric ceremonies are performed by Mormons deemed worthy to enter. Performed in these buildings are wedding ceremonies, sealings, washing and anointings, endowments, and baptisms for the dead, whereby those who have died are given an opportunity to receive Mormonism in the spirit world. About 98% of what occurs in Mormon temples is for the dead.

CHRISTIAN: There was only one temple, which was found in Jerusalem. It was a place where animal sacrifices were made on behalf of the sins of the people. The Bible never suggests that these buildings were used for marriage ceremonies or baptisms as taught by the LDS Church. Whereas *worthiness* is required to enter a Mormon temple, it was a sense of *unworthiness* that caused the penitent Jew to enter the Jerusalem temple.

See *ORDINANCES, TEMPLE RECOMMEND.*

TEMPLE GARMENTS:

See *GARMENTS OF THE HOLY PRIESTHOOD.*

TEMPLE MORMON:

A member of the Mormon Church who has been found worthy to enter and participate in temple ceremonies.

See *TEMPLE.*

TEMPLE RECOMMEND:

A card that allows a member of the Mormon Church access to a temple. This is given only after a strict interview with his or her bishop and only if the applicant is in good standing in the church.

TERRESTRIAL KINGDOM:

The second highest Mormon heaven reserved for honorable people who did not embrace Mormonism.

TESTIMONY, MORMON:

A strong feeling on the part of Mormons that tells them Mormonism is true. This testimony is also known as a burning in the bosom and usually consists of "knowing" the Mormon Church to be the true Church, Joseph Smith to be a true prophet of God, and the *Book of Mormon* to be God's word.

TESTIMONY MEETING:

A sacrament meeting where members bear their testimonies.

See *SACRAMENT MEETING.*

THREE DEGREES OF GLORY:
One of three places where mankind will spend eternity according to the works performed in this life.

See CELESTIAL KINGDOM, TERRESTRIAL KINGDOM, TELESTIAL KINGDOM.

TIMES AND SEASONS:
A monthly Mormon periodical printed during the time when the LDS Church was headquartered in Nauvoo, Illinois. Edited by Ebenezer Robinson and Don Carlos Smith (Joseph Smith's brother). Its first issue appeared in November 1839.

TRANSGRESSION:
See SIN.

TRINITY:
MORMON: Three separate gods: the Father, Son, and Holy Ghost make up the Mormon godhead. They are "one God" only in the sense that they are united in the attributes of perfection. *"Each occupies space and is and can be in but one place at one time, but each has power and influence that is everywhere present. The oneness of the Gods is the same unity that should exist among the saints"* (*Mormon Doctrine*, p. 319). In a speech given at B.Y.U. in 1984, Mormon Apostle Bruce McConkie called the evangelical Christian view of the Trinity the *"first greatest heresy."*

CHRISTIAN: One God, which is comprised of the Father, Son, and Holy Spirit. Whereas Mormonism states they are three separate Gods, Christians maintain the triune godhead neither confounds the Persons nor divides the substance [essence]. In the words of the Athanasian Creed: *"For there is one Person of the Father: another of the Son: and another of the Holy Ghost. But the godhead of the Father, of the Son, and of the Holy Ghost is all one: the Glory equal, the Majesty coeternal."*

TRIPLE COMBINATION:
The *Book of Mormon, Doctrine and Covenants,* and *Pearl of Great Price* bound together as one book.

URIM AND THUMMIM:

MORMON: Two stones in silver bows, which were buried with the Golden Plates. These special stones were also called seer stones or interpreters. Joseph Smith used the Urim and Thummim to translate the *Book of Mormon* from Reformed Egyptian to English.

CHRISTIAN: First mentioned in Exodus 28:30, the Urim and Thummim were to be placed in the breastplate of judgment worn by Aaron and the future high priests. The Bible does not exactly say what constituted the Urim and Thummim.

See BOOK OF MORMON, REFORMED EGYPTIAN, SEER STONE.

VIRGIN BIRTH:

MORMON: The physical union between God (Elohim) and Mary. Mary was a virgin only in the sense that she did not have sexual relations with a mortal man; however, Mormon leaders have taught that she did have sexual relations with an immortal man of body, parts, and passions. *"God the Father became the literal father of Jesus Christ. Jesus was born of a mortal mother and an immortal father"* (*Gospel Principles*, p. 57). Bruce McConkie taught that Jesus *"is the Son of God in the same sense and way that we are the sons of mortal fathers. It is just that simple"* (*The Promised Messiah*, p. 468).

CHRISTIAN: Mary was overshadowed by the Holy Ghost (Matthew 1:18). Jesus was conceived without any physical relations.

WARD:

A local Mormon congregation. Several wards form a stake.

See BISHOPRIC, STAKE.

WASHING AND ANOINTING:

An ordinance performed in Mormon temples whereby the participant wears nothing but a poncho-like shield as he/she is ceremoniously washed with water and anointed with oil by a temple worker. The participant's head, ears, nose, lips, neck, shoulders, back, breasts, arms and hands, loins, legs and feet are washed with water and then the ceremony is repeated with oil. Men are separated from the women during this rite.

WENTWORTH LETTER:
A letter written by Joseph Smith at the request of John Wentworth, editor of the *Chicago Democrat*. The 1842 letter briefly gave an account of Joseph Smith's background and his new movement. The letter concluded with a list of Smith's beliefs, which has since come to be known as the *Articles of Faith*.

See ARTICLES OF FAITH.

WITNESSES:
Eleven men who testified to the authenticity of the *Book of Mormon*. Divided into two categories, the three witnesses were Joseph Smith's close associates Oliver Cowdery, David Whitmer, and Martin Harris. Later, eight more men were asked to give their testimonies. These eight witnesses were Christian Whitmer, Jacob Whitmer, Peter Whitmer, John Whitmer, Hiram Page, Joseph Smith, Sen., Hyrum Smith, and Samuel H. Smith. Each of the three witnesses and five of the eight witnesses were later excommunicated from the LDS Church. Their testimonies were originally found in the back of the 1830 edition of the *Book of Mormon* and are located in the front of every modern edition.

WOODRUFF, WILFORD (1807–1898):
Became Mormonism's fourth president in 1889, following the death of John Taylor.

WORD OF WISDOM:
A Mormon health law found in *Doctrine & Covenants*, Section 89, which tells Mormons to abstain from hot drinks, tobacco, and alcoholic beverages. Obedience to this health law is one of the requirements to receive a temple recommend. Those who keep these sayings are promised that *"the destroying angel shall pass by them"* (89:18, 21).

See TEMPLE RECOMMEND.

YOUNG, BRIGHAM (1801–1877):
Became Mormonism's second president in 1847, following the death of Joseph Smith.

ZION:

MORMON: A name that has had a number of different meanings throughout Mormon history. Zion is a name given by the Lord to his saints. *"And the Lord called his people Zion"* (Moses 7:18). Zion was the name given to Jackson County, Missouri, in a number of Joseph Smith's revelations (*D & C* 58:49; 62:4). In 1831, Joseph Smith said Jackson County would come to be known as the New Jerusalem (*D & C* 45:66–67). In 1844, Smith said that the Land of Zion comprised all of North and South America (*Teachings of the Prophet Joseph Smith*, p. 362).

CHRISTIAN: Also spelled Sion. It was the highest and southwest-ernmost hill in Jerusalem. Also used in the Bible to describe the heavenly New Jerusalem (Revelation 14:1).

BIBLIOGRAPHY

Andersen, Darl. *Soft Answers to Hard Questions.* Mesa, Arizona: Darl Andersen, 1989.

Archer, Gleason. *A Survey of the Old Testament.* Chicago, Illinois: Moody Press, 1964.

A Sure Foundation: Answers to Difficult Gospel Questions. Salt Lake City, Utah: Deseret Book Company, 1988.

Backman, Milton V. *The First Vision.* Salt Lake City, Utah: Bookcraft Publishers, 1971.

Beckwith, Francis. "Philosophical Problems With the Mormon Concept of God," *Christian Research Journal,* Spring 1992, p. 28.

Benson, Ezra Taft. *The Teachings of Ezra Taft Benson.* Salt Lake City, Utah: Bookcraft, 1988.

Bergera, Gary James, editor. *Line Upon Line.* Salt Lake City, Utah: Signature Books, 1989.

Berret, William. *The Restored Church,* 15th ed. Salt Lake City, Utah: Deseret Book Company, 1973.

Bevan, Edwyn Robert. *Later Greek Religion.* New York: E. P. Dutton & Co., 1927.

Bromiley, G. W., editor. *The International Standard Bible Encyclopedia,* 4 volumes. Grand Rapids, Michigan: William B. Eerdmans Publishing Company, 1979.

Bruce, F. F. *The Book of the Acts.* Grand Rapids: William G. Eerdmans, 1988.

Bruce, F. F. *The Hard Sayings of Jesus.* Downers Grove, Illinois: Intervarsity Press, 1983.

Cannon, George Q. *Gospel Truth.* Salt Lake City, Utah: Deseret Book Company, 1987.

Carver, James A. *Answering an Ex-Mormon Critic.* Sandy, Utah: Mormon Miscellaneous, 1983.

Church News. Select issues from the weekly LDS newspaper, published by the *Deseret News.* Salt Lake City, Utah: *Deseret News.*

Clark, George Edward. *Why I Believe.* Salt Lake City, Utah: Bookcraft, 1952.

Cox, James B. *How to Qualify for the Celestial Kingdom Today.* Riverton, Utah: The Ensign Publishing Company, 1984.

Deseret News 1993–1994 Church Almanac. Salt Lake City, Utah: *Deseret News,* 1992.

Doctrine and Covenants Student Manual. Salt Lake City, Utah: The Church of Jesus Christ of Latter-day Saints, 1981.

Edersheim, Alfred. *The Temple.* Grand Rapids, Michigan: William B. Eerdmans Publishing Company, 1976.

Encyclopedia of Mormonism. New York, New York: Macmillan Publishing Company.

The Ensign. Select issues from the monthly magazine published by the LDS Church. Salt Lake City, Utah: The Church of Jesus Christ of Latter-day Saints.

Geisler, Norman and William Nix. *A General Introduction to the Bible.* Chicago, Illinois: Moody Press, 1968.

Gospel Principles. Salt Lake City, Utah: Published by the Church of Jesus Christ of Latter-day Saints, 1985.

Graf, Fritz. *Greek Mythology.* Baltimore, Maryland: John Hopkins University Press, 1993.

Green, Doyle L. and Randall L. Green. *Meet the Mormons.* Salt Lake City, Utah: Deseret Book Company, 1965.

Hunter, Milton R. *The Gospel Through the Ages.* Salt Lake City, Utah: Stevens and Wallis, Inc., 1945.

Joseph Smith's 'New Translation' of the Bible. Independence, Missouri: Herald Publishing House, 1970.

Kaiser, Walter, Jr. *More Hard Sayings of the Old Testament.* Downers Grove, Illinois: InterVarsity Press, 1992.

Kenyon, Sir Frederick G. *Our Bible and Ancient Manuscripts.* New York: Harper and Brother, 1941.

Kerényi, C. *The Gods and the Greeks.* London: Thames and Hudson, 1951.

Kimball, Edward L., editor. *The Teachings of Spencer W. Kimball.* Salt Lake City, Utah: Bookcraft, Inc., 1982.

Kimball, Spencer W. *The Miracle of Forgiveness.* Salt Lake City, Utah: Bookcraft, Inc., 1969.

Kimball, Spencer W. *Repentance Brings Forgiveness.* Salt Lake City, Utah: The Church of Jesus Christ of Latter-day Saints, 1984. (This LDS Church tract is an adaptation of an address given at BYU, May 4, 1954.)

Kirkham. Francis W. *A New Witness for Christ in America,* Vol. I., 3rd ed.. Salt Lake City, Utah: Utah Printing Colo., 1960.

Lee, Rex. *What Do Mormons Believe?* Salt Lake City, Utah: Deseret Book Company, 1992.

Living Prophets for a Living Church. Salt Lake City, Utah: Church of Jesus Christ of Latter-day Saints, 1974.

McConkie, Bruce R. *Mormon Doctrine,* 2nd ed. Salt Lake City, Utah: Bookcraft, Inc., 1966.

McConkie, Bruce R. *The Mortal Messiah.* Salt Lake City, Utah: Deseret Book Company, 1982.

McConkie, Bruce R. *A New Witness to the Articles of Faith.* Salt Lake City, Utah: Deseret Book Company, 1985.

McConkie, Bruce R. *The Promised Messiah.* Salt Lake City, Utah: Deseret Book Company, 1978.

McDowell, Josh. *Evidence That Demands a Verdict.* San Bernardino, California: Here's Life Publishers, Inc., 1986.

McKeever, Bill. *Answering Mormons' Questions.* Minneapolis, Minnesota: Bethany House Publishers, 1991.

Millennial Star. An official LDS publication, which was published in the British Isles from 1840–1970, and later became *The Ensign.*

Nibley, Hugh. *An Approach to the Book of Mormon,* 2nd ed. Salt Lake City, Utah: Deseret Book Company, 1978.

Nibley, Hugh. *Since Cumorah.* Salt Lake City, Utah: Deseret Book Company, 1986.

Petersen, Mark E. *As Translated Correctly.* Salt Lake City, Utah: Deseret Book Company, 1966.

Peterson, Daniel C. and Stephen D. Ricks. *Offenders for a Word: How Anti-Mormons Play Word Games to Attack the Latter-day Saints.* Salt Lake City, Utah: Aspen Books, 1992.

Pinset, John. *Greek Mythology.* New York: Peter Bedick Books, 1982.

Pratt, Orson. *The Seer.* Reprint of newspapers published between January 1853 and August 1854.

Pratt, Orson. *A Series of Pamphlets,* Liverpool, England: 1851.

Pratt, Parley P. *Key to the Science of Theology: A Voice of Warning.* Salt Lake City: Desert Book Company, 1978.

Quinn, D. Michael. *Early Mormonism and the Magic World View.* Salt Lake City, Utah: Signature Books, 1987.

Richards, LeGrand. *A Marvelous Work and a Wonder.* Salt Lake City, Utah: Deseret Book Company, 1979.

Roberts, B. H., compiler. *A Comprehensive History of the Church of Jesus Christ of Latter-day Saints,* 6 volumes. Provo, Utah: Brigham Young University Press, 1965.

Robison, Parker Pratt, compiler. *Writings of Parley Parker Pratt.* Salt Lake City, Utah: Deseret News Press, 1952.

Robinson, Stephen E. *Are Mormons Christians?* Salt Lake City, Utah: Bookcraft, Inc., 1991.

Ryrie, Charles C. *Does It Really Matter What You Believe?* Garland, Texas: American Tract Society, 1993.

Search These Commandments: Melchizedek Priesthood Personal Study Guide. Salt Lake City, Utah: The Church of Jesus Christ of Latter-day Saints, 1984.

Shields, Steven L. *Divergent Paths of the Restoration,* 4th ed. Los Angeles: Restoration Research, 1990.

Smith, Joseph, Jr. The *Book of Mormon.* Church of Jesus Christ of Latter-day Saints, 1830 and 1981.

Smith, Joseph, Jr. *Doctrine and Covenants.* Church of Jesus Christ of Latter-day Saints, 1981.

Smith, Joseph, Jr. *History of the Church of Jesus Christ of Latter-day Saints,* 6 volumes. Introduction and notes by B. H. Roberts. Salt Lake City, Utah: Deseret Book Company, 1973.

Smith, Joseph, Jr. *Inspired Version of the Holy Scriptures.* Independence, Missouri: Herald Publishing House, 1955.

Smith, Joseph, Jr. The *Pearl of Great Price*. Church of Jesus Christ of Latter-day Saints, 1981.

Smith, Joseph F. *Gospel Doctrine*. Salt Lake City, Utah: Deseret Book Company, 1977.

Smith, Joseph Fielding. *Answers to Gospel Questions*, 5 volumes. Salt Lake City, Utah: Deseret Book Company, 1979.

Smith, Joseph Fielding. *Doctrines of Salvation*, 3 volumes. Salt Lake City, Utah: Bookcraft, 1976.

Smith, Joseph Fielding. *Man: His Origin and Destiny*, 2nd ed. Salt Lake City, Utah: Deseret Book Company, 1954.

Smith, Joseph Fielding, compiler. *Teachings of the Prophet Joseph Smith*. Salt Lake City, Utah: Deseret Book Company, 1977.

Smith, Joseph Fielding. *The Way to Perfection*. Salt Lake City, Utah: Deseret Book Company, 1975.

Smith, Lucy Mack. *History of Joseph Smith by His Mother, Lucy Mack Smith*. Salt Lake City, Utah: Steven E Wallis, Inc., 1945.

Sperry, Sidney. *The Problems of the Book of Mormon*. Salt Lake City, Utah: Bookcraft, 1964.

Sunstone. Select issues. Salt Lake City, Utah: The Sunstone Foundation.

Talmage, James E. *The Articles of Faith*. Salt Lake City, Utah: The Church of Jesus Christ of Latter-day Saints, 1982.

Talmage, James E. *Jesus the Christ*. Salt Lake City, Utah: Deseret Book Company, 1977.

Tanner, Jerald and Sandra. *Mormonism—Shadow or Reality?* 4th edition. Salt Lake City, Utah: Utah Lighthouse Ministry, 1982.

Tanner, Jerald and Sandra, compilers. *Joseph Smith's 1832 Account of His Early Life*. Salt Lake City, Utah: Modern Microfilm Company, 1979.

Teachings of Lorenzo Snow, The. Compiled by Clyde J. Williams. Salt Lake City, Utah: Bookcraft, 1984.

Times and Seasons. A six-volume series that contains copies of the LDS newspaper printed between November 1839 and February 15, 1846.

Walters, Wesley. *Joseph Smith's Bainbridge, N.Y., Court Trials*. Salt Lake City, Utah: Utah Lighthouse Ministry, n.d.

Walters, Wesley. *New Light on Mormon Origins*. El Cajon, California: Mormonism Research Minstry, 1990.

Watt, G. D., compiler. *Journal of Discourses*, 26 volumes. Liverpool, England: 1854–1886.

White, James. "Mormon Scholars Defend Their Church: A Review and Rebuttal of Offenders for a Word," *Pros Apologian*, Spring 1993, pp. 5–6.

Whitmer, David. *An Address to All Believers in Christ*. Richmond, Missouri: David Whitmer, 1887.

Widtsoe, John. *Priesthood and Church Government*. Salt Lake City, Utah: Deseret Book Company, 1967.

Widtsoe, John A. *Evidences and Reconciliations*. Salt Lake City, Utah: Bookcraft, Inc., 1987.

INDEX